'An honest, compassionate celebration of style and creativity. This is what to read if you love clothes, women and the planet and you want to be inspired to do right by all of them.' Daisy Buchanan

'Offers honest and realistic advice . . . Bravo will inspire you to repair, recycle and give old items a new lease of life, all without sacrificing your style, and the planet.' *Stylist*

'A funny, achievable guide to reducing our fabric footprint, and covers swapping, mending, washing less and, most importantly, resisting the urge to shop.' *Observer*

'A witty and persuasive book . . . Bravo writes with the wry verve of a viral tweet [and] shares her style secrets, from secondhand shopping to a good-luck dress.' *Telegraph*

'A guilt-free guide that will change the way you think about clothing for the better.' *Independent*

'For anyone wanting to change up their fashion ways, this book is invaluable.' Katherine Ormerod

'Lauren is an important voice . . . she encourages us all to see a future full of exciting styled looks no matter what our budget.' Caryn Franklin

'This book will educate you as well as make you laugh.' *Stellar*

'*How To Break Up With Fast Fashion* offers realistic advice on repairing and recycling your wardrobe, encouraging readers to embrace more sustainable ways of shopping.' *Country & Town House*

'Brilliant tips.' *Who What Wear*

Lauren Bravo is a freelance journalist who writes about fashion, popular culture, food, travel and feminism, for places like *Grazia*, *Refinery29*, *Cosmopolitan*, *Stylist*, the *Telegraph* and the *Guardian*. She was *The Pool*'s 'Wardrobe Stories' columnist. Her first book, *What Would the Spice Girls Do?* was published by Transworld in 2018. In 2019, Lauren went on a year-long fast fashion ban. She also volunteers in a charity shop once a week (partly to get first dibs on all the best clothes). Lauren is on Twitter and Instagram as @laurenbravo.

How to Break Up with Fast Fashion

LAUREN BRAVO

For Mum and Dad,
who've had this figured out all along

First published in 2020 by HEADLINE HOME
an imprint of HEADLINE PUBLISHING GROUP

First published in paperback in 2021

1

Cataloguing in Publication Data is available from the British Library

ISBN 978 1 4722 6776 4
e-ISBN 978 1 4722 6773 3

Typeset in 9.75/15.25pt Versailles by Jouve (UK), Milton Keynes

Printed and bound in Great Britain by Clays Ltd, Elcograf S.p.A.

Headline's policy is to use papers that are natural, renewable and recyclable
products and made from wood grown in well-managed forests and other
controlled sources. The logging and manufacturing processes are expected
to conform to the environmental regulations of the country of origin.

HEADLINE PUBLISHING GROUP
An Hachette UK Company
Carmelite House
50 Victoria Embankment
London
EC4Y 0DZ

www.headline.co.uk
www.hachette.co.uk

CONTENTS

Part Three: The Rebound

AN ACCESSORY TO THIS BOOK

It's an unavoidable truth that a non-fiction book, especially one full of facts and stats like this one, tends to be anchored to the point in time at which it was written. And it's fair to say that since I finished writing this book, in mid-2019, *a lot* has happened . . . You remember, you were there.

Over the past year I have watched the conversation around sustainable and ethical fashion grow louder and more nuanced, more impatient and more exciting. We've seen some brands make strides to do better, and many continue to fall embarrassingly short.

The coronavirus pandemic has served to further expose the deep, ugly inequality which runs through so many areas of our society – and fashion is no exception. Billions of pounds' worth of orders from garment factories were cancelled, with many huge corporations refusing to pay what they owed – another devastating blow to some of the poorest and most exploited workers in the world. In the midst of a global crisis, fast fashion has shown its true colours, and they aren't cute.

Around the same time, many of those same companies were posting black squares on Instagram. We've seen

brands falling over themselves to make their on-trend statements in support of the Black Lives Matter movement, but
few, if any, have acknowledged the part they play in that
oppression. Let's be clear here: fashion has been built on
the back of white supremacy, colonialism and cultural
appropriation. Lots of us were shocked when it came out
that popular brands (including 'ethical' ones) were guilty of
racially profiling their customers and racially discriminat-
ing against their staff. We shouldn't have been shocked. We
should have been paying attention.

As a result, I've made a couple of changes to the original
text of this book. I've taken out one sustainable brand that
has lost my respect, and added several black-owned brands
that are so much more deserving of that support. I'm sorry
they weren't there to begin with.

In all likelihood, yet more will have happened in the gap
between me writing this note and you reading it. Time tends
to work that way. And as much as I wish I could come to
each of your houses with a red pen and update the book on
a weekly basis, my publishers won't let me do that.

So instead, I'd like to say: please read this in the way it
was always intended – as a jumping-off point for your own
journey. When you've finished it, don't stop there. Seek out
the brilliant activists who have been banging this drum for
years. Learn more, listen more and join the fight as it continues. That's certainly what I'll be doing.

INTRODUCTION

Like so many relationship dramas, it all kicked off on New Year's Eve.

While everyone else is on the Aldi champagne and pan-Asian party nibbles, I am on ASOS, scrolling like a woman possessed.

The next day, 1 January, I am giving up fast fashion for a year. A whole year – or #notnewyear, as my friend Daisy has cannily branded it – without the high street, without online hauls, without multiple weekly visits from Joseph the DPD man. This, I realise, as I sit on my parents' sofa scrolling through 4,641 midi dresses while the clock inches closer to midnight and Jools Holland loads the confetti canon, is my last hurrah.

I buy five dresses. I buy them hastily and hungrily, clicking 'add to basket' on anything passable that hasn't sold out in my size. I shop in the way I have so many other times over the years: palms clammy, pupils dilated, on a mission to see every single option before more are unleashed. One more page. One more search. One more scroll. I shop as though I am a donkey and the perfect outfit is a carrot, bobbing forever just out of reach.

I've been this way for years. It's the way I shopped the afternoon before the first mufti day of secondary school, haring around Mark One for something to save me from a fate worse than my C&A fleece. I did a similar shop the day before my cousin's wedding, aged fifteen, tramping across Brighton with my mum until the shops started closing and I had vetoed every sensible knee-length dress in the city. I've done it before practically every wedding I've ever been to, in fact, which as a thirty-something woman with what can only be described as a 'friend-retention problem', is many. Twenty-six. Twenty-six weddings and almost as many frantic sprints around Accessorize for emergency clutch bags.

Throughout my life, clothes have been my passion and the acquisition of clothes my most devoted hobby. I've shopped like it is going out of fashion. I've shopped to celebrate and commiserate. Holidays, Christmas parties, birthdays, Tuesdays. I've shopped because the weather has changed, and I've shopped because it hasn't. I've shopped out of boredom, out of stress, out of friendship, out of love, and as a way to crystallise happy memories I was scared might otherwise slip away.

Incidentally, you could replace the word 'shopped' above with 'eaten' and every sentence would remain true. Clothes, like food, can be a baseline need or an all-consuming passion, but something that we all have to engage with to a lesser or greater extent. Whether we consider ourselves a

fashionista or just an impartial bystander, we can't really –
nudity and prison excepted – opt out.

Some of the shopping has been great. That's partly why I've
carried on doing it, and not given up to live in a hessian
sack with holes for arms. I've had those fantastic, fatalistic
shopping trips; the ones where the stars align and so do all
the buttons. Where friends applaud and strangers bound
across a changing room to tell you that you HAVE to buy it,
oh my god. Where the jacket the shop assistant thought was
sold out is unearthed magically in your size from a dusty
corner of a stock room, in precisely the time it's taken for
you to decide it might be your soul jacket, your destiny, the
One True Jacket to rule them all.

I have danced out of shops cradling a carrier bag like a new-
born baby, beaming at everyone because I just can't believe
my luck. I've lovingly stroked a corner of fabric the whole
way home, delighted in the decisive stretch aaaaaand *snap*
of removing the tag in my bedroom. It's a blessed ritual.
One of life's small victories. I hereby declare you *a keeper.*

Of course, the One True Jacket ends up relegated to a lower
peg a few months later, because you're bored and a button
fell off and you had your head turned by another sexy piece
of outerwear. But that's the thing about love stories. They
never show what happens after you waltz off into the
sunset.

A few days after my New Year's haul, already feeling the
first queasy pangs of withdrawal, the parcel arrived. I tore

it open and hoofed them all onto my bed. There they were, my last hurrah, now a creased heap of floral polyester. I tried them on. And in the time-honoured tradition of online shopping, I rejected them, one by one. Too wafty. Too clingy. Weird ruffles. Bad sleeves. Back in the bag you go, pal.

I kept one dress out of the five, mainly because I couldn't bear to end up back where I'd started: at New Dress Neutral. The one I kept, a high-necked floral situation by Monki made, oddly, of swimsuit fabric, quickly became my go-to dress over the next month or so. I reached for it again and again, the only thing I found myself wanting to wear every morning, and eventually I realised this was not because it was especially gorgeous (see: swimsuit fabric) or looked especially good *on me*, but purely because it was the newest thing that I owned. And newness is everything.

The pursuit of the new is human instinct. It's what we do, and always have done – we push forward, we innovate, we get bored and start sniffing around for the next source of excitement; the next micro-hit of dopamine. Once upon a time it might have been a woolly mammoth carcass. Now it's the tiny blinking notification of an email saying our order's been dispatched.

Psychologists call it habituation: 'the diminishing of an innate response to a frequently repeated stimulus.'[1] The more we see something, the less it thrills us. The outfit we loved so much a few months ago becomes 'this old thing', shrugged on begrudgingly and apologised for at parties.

But we can't lay all this at biology's door. In recent years, we've supercharged our pursuit of novelty and with it created a monster. A great, mutant monster with one hand in our wallet at all times. Fast fashion.

'Fast' fashion has no official definition, but it's characterised by two things: low prices and relentless pace. It cycles through trends so rapidly that transience has become almost the defining trend of a generation. Our parents had bellbottoms and platforms, our grandparents had circle skirts and spats; we have a constantly moving conveyor belt of possessions, and the urge to replace them at the drop of a hat. (One of those wide-brimmed straw hats, owned by every single influencer but never seen on an actual head.)

Global clothing production has roughly doubled in just fifteen years.[2] Startling, isn't it? At current growth rates it will take two hundred years for the world's population to double, and yet somehow we've produced twice as many clothes in the time since Facebook was invented.

And with the breakneck rise of fast fashion, our habituation has become capitulation too. While the industry churns out more than we can ever possibly buy or wear, it also ploughs billions of pounds into convincing us that it's our duty to try. These days when we're bored of our clothes, the solution isn't adding a jazzy belt or changing our hair – it's buying a whole new outfit. Same goes for boredom in general. Those of us who love fashion have come to use it as a multi-purpose cure-all for everything from heartache to headache. It's the old trope of 'retail therapy' taken to an all-too-literal conclusion, a place where buying non-essential shit can be classed as vital self-care. Got a vague itch of dissatisfaction you can't quite put your finger on? Shop it better! Why the hell not?

Except we know why not.

Right now we know both more than we want to, and less than we need to. Overwhelmed with clutter, both physical and mental, we've started to look around and ask: have we reached saturation point? Is it possible we have ... *too much stuff*?

The answer is yes, obviously. It's been yes for years. But we had our hands too full of returns to notice.

Wising up to the reality of fast fashion has been both a slow dawning of realisation and a series of short, sharp shocks. When the Rana Plaza building in Dhaka, Bangladesh collapsed on 24 April 2013, killing 1,138 garment workers and injuring some 2,500 more, it marked the darkest day the industry has ever seen and shone a light on the true cost of our clothes; not in pounds and pence, but human life and suffering.

It wasn't that we had no idea the workers making our clothes were badly paid – in Bangladesh it's as little as $37 a month, some of the lowest legal wages in the world[3] – but, truthfully, before that day and the conversations it generated, most of us had been able to avoid thinking about them. Those people. Those women, because it is mostly women. Without putting faces, voices or stories to the things that we wore, it was easier to pretend our clothes were merely picked off trees, or born fully-formed and folded on the display table. As Rana Plaza crumbled, so did a little part of the opacity that had shielded our conscience for so long.

Now 'transparency' is the buzzword and visible supply chains are the goal. The tragedy inspired action, such as the formation of Fashion Revolution, a global not-for-profit organisation that campaigns for massive reform across the industry. They designated 24 April as Fashion Revolution Day, and over the past six years they and other groups have united in acts of 'pro-fashion' protest – not telling us to quit shopping altogether, but encouraging us all to ask #whomademyclothes: what were they paid and how were they treated? It was a watershed moment, though it wasn't enough to turn the tide. Yet.

For the global fashion industry, the year following the Rana Plaza disaster was the most profitable of all time. Even as the rubble was cleared and the death toll rose, the world carried on shopping. We shopped and shopped, and when our wardrobes overflowed and our floordrobes became unbearable, we threw stuff away to make room for more.

Every year in the UK, an estimated 300,000 tonnes of used clothing now ends up in landfill[4] – although the word 'used' is disputable seeing as garments are reportedly worn on average just seven times before they're thrown, more often than not, in the bin.[5] In 2019, Brits spent an estimated £2.7 billion on clothes worn only once – including £700 million on 11 million summer outfits that didn't make it beyond the duration of a single holiday.[6]

Fashion is widely reported as one of the most polluting industries in the world. Some say second only to oil; some say more like third, fifth or sixth – it's hard to know for sure. But we do know that Boohoo and Missguided sell dresses for less than the cost of a Pret sandwich. And in an economy where so many basic requirements seem to be escalating wildly out of reach – homes, transport, education, lunch – it's hardly surprising that we're snapping up the bargains where we find them. It's even less surprising when they unravel from the hems a week later.

It's not just a question of thrift. As fashion gets cheaper and cheaper, somehow we're also shopping like we're richer than we are. Instagram tells us we should all be celebrities, with single-wear wardrobes to match. Advertising continues to dance the merry dance it has for decades: a kind of retail negging whereby they tell us that we're inadequate, sell us clothes to soothe the sting, then chase us round the internet with anything we dare to leave behind in a basket. The lines between 'want' and 'need' have never felt so blurry.

Back in 1932, the pioneering ad executive Earnest Elmo Calkins (the 'other' Elmo) declared, 'Goods fall into two classes: those that we use, such as motor cars and safety razors, and those that we use up, such as toothpaste or soda biscuits. Consumer engineering must see to it that we use up the kind of goods we now merely use.'

Consumer engineering saw to it all right. As prices plummet so does quality, and so does longevity, and so does our willingness to keep trotting out the same saggy £17.99 dress for every social occasion. Clothing has become what marketeers call 'FMCG' – Fast-moving Consumer Goods – although many tubes of toothpaste last longer than our shopping trophies do.

Where once brands released four collections a year in line with the season, now it's often fifty-two or more, trends that are going, going, GONE before we can even decide we like them. To keep up, we've become sartorial commitment-phobes, taking our clothes out for dinner and never calling them again. We're ghosting our Ghost. Calling full time on our Whistles. And all the while, the planet groans under the weight of twice as many clothes as were produced just fifteen years ago.

Funnily enough, fifteen years is roughly the amount of time it takes for a fashion trend to resurface. Back in 2004, I was wearing a lot of flares, corduroy, statement blouses and velvet blazers. Right now I am also wearing a lot of flares, corduroy, statement blouses and velvet blazers, only *very slightly* different ones. Fashion, and I'll say this again although I won't always mean it, is a bastard. The one you lavish affection and time and energy on, believing they love you too, only to realise after years of tears and heartache that you were putting in more than you ever got back.

Of course, the toxic relationship analogy is painfully on point. From carbon emissions to river pollution to cotton pesticides to plastic microfibres ending up in our tap water, barely a week goes by without another miserable statistic, another bleak reminder that there are only a handful of years left to stop the climate change juggernaut before . . . well, we usually stop reading at that part because it's terrifying.

But it's galvanising, too. Just now it feels as though we're waking up from decades of sleepwalking to the impact of all this accumulation – on the planet, on humanity and on our own mental health. And if there's one thing working in sustainability's favour, it's that trends catch on quick.

Just ask David Attenborough, everyone's favourite influencer. After the veteran broadcaster showed the scale of plastic pollution in the world's oceans in *that* episode of Blue Planet II, there was a tidal wave of behaviour change. The phrase 'single-use plastic' entered the vernacular and the idea took hold like contraband clingfilm. Suddenly it was out with disposable coffee cups, down with excessive packaging, and woe betide the bartender who tried to give us a plastic straw. Some 88 per cent of viewers adjusted their shopping habits as a result of the episode (or at least claimed they had in a survey by Waitrose,[7] which admittedly isn't quite the same thing), and 53 per cent of UK and US consumers have reduced the amount of plastic they use in the year since.[8]

Whether it's progress enough to make a difference remains to be seen, but it still felt heartening to see the shift happening before our eyes. It was *something*. And we all want to feel like we can do something.

Now fashion is experiencing a similar shakedown, and not a season too soon. The 'Marie Kondo effect' has charity shops flourishing while traditional retail flounders. Minimalism has been enjoying a comeback, as we 'edit' and 'streamline' everything from our wardrobes to our social lives in a bid to ease our conscience and soothe our frazzled brains. And the shops are paying attention, as well they should. Some of the biggest high-street retailers are now launching 'eco' collections, urging us to recycle clothes in exchange for discounts, and waving their code of conduct around for all to see.

Meanwhile, new indie brands fall over themselves to one-up each other on ethics and innovation. Trainers made of tyres! Swimsuits made of fishing nets! Dresses made of egg boxes and sticky-backed plastic! Sweatshirts that will never wear out, and jeans that will never wear in. It's brilliant, exciting, polarising and confusing. Is cotton good or evil? Is H&M allowed now? Did sweatshirts ever wear out anyway? Isn't 'vegan leather' just what our mums would sniffily call 'not even leather'? And if £200 is 'just what a dress ought to cost', then what happens if we don't have £200? Sustainability can often feel like the preserve of the lucky, wealthy, skinny, educated few, even while they're telling us how badly it affects *us all*. There are so many stats. So much conflicting advice. So much to learn, and so hard to know where to start. It's easy to get overwhelmed and bury our heads in the sand, and by 'sand' I mean cheap polyester.

But while we might not know exactly what or how to change, we know that we need to change something. That's why you're reading this, isn't it? And why I'm writing it. It's time to take our foot off the pedal, get off the high street super-highway, or at least steer ourselves safely into a ditch. Time to have the difficult conversations, and the tantrums. I don't have all the answers, but I do have plenty more mixed metaphors, so buckle up.

For now, my own relationship with fast fashion is estranged but far from over. I'm at the fragile stage; still gazing wistfully through the windows of & Other Stories, still catching wafts of its scent in my cupboards and falling into nostalgic reverie. I'm determined to move on and seek closure, but I can't promise there will never be a drunken reunion or a masochistic relapse. I can't promise I will never call up fast fashion at 2am to sob over what went wrong.

Still, I hope that makes me a better candidate to write this book than a person who quit shopping so long ago they can barely remember the taste. Not only have I shopped *like* it was a career, I have made it one. In my time, I've written for budget fashion brands, high-end designers and supermarkets. I've churned out 800 words on why we should all buy a skirt two inches longer than last year's, and I've believed almost every one of them. I've never truly been an industry insider – the only time I ever went to London Fashion Week I trod in dog shit on the way and I've never quite shaken off that omen – but even from my place among the cheap seats in the back, I've still done my bit to feed the beast. I hold my hands up; I am a hypocrite. But I'm a hopeful one.

Because while fashion got us into this mess, I like to think fashion could also get us out. After all, Disney characters and posh dogs excepted, we're the only species in the world to wear clothes. They're at once both an unavoidable, functional necessity and an outlet for pleasure and art. If what we love about fashion is the good stuff, the creativity, the self-expression, the thrill of being swept up in a cultural moment, then that force of communal spirit could surely power us all in a new direction. A fairer, more sustainable one. Slower, steadier. Backwards, if need be.

We need to do it soon, but we don't need to do it alone. Like the friend who turns up after a break-up, packs all your pants into a suitcase and strongarms you to the pub, yelling, 'YOU'RE TOO GOOD FOR THEM,' I want this book to be a companion, not a critic. I also hope it'll help us both unpick that relationship, reprogramme our 'must-buy!' mindset and trace those urges back to their source. Be it the patriarchy, PMS, or the misguided belief that a person can never have too many Breton tops (they definitely can).

Along the way I've spoken to academics, activists, sustainability advocates and fashion influencers, in a bid to understand things better. There's a fast-growing community around slow fashion, and it's been heartening to see how many people want to share their insights and advice. We've been practising conspicuous consumption since the days we carried our PE kits in Jane Norman carrier bags, but now I want to believe we can egg each other on to reverse those habits, escape the co-dependency, and find new, better ways to celebrate our love of clothes.

Although those ways won't all be the same. We can't wear everything at once, much as some of us have tried, and we can't *do* everything at once either. For some of us, the best plan of action might be buying five quality items and wearing them all for a decade. For others, it'll be trawling charity shops the way we used to hit up Primark. For some it might be threading a needle for the first time since school or swapping and selling the clothes we used to bin and burn.

I don't know everything, but I do know there is no single *right* way to break up with fast fashion.

After all, as Paul Simon once sang, there are fifty ways to leave your lover. You just cut up your cards, Barb. Learn to sew, Flo. Go secondhand, Suzanne. Just listen to me.

Get yourself on eBay, Mae. Why don't you donate, Kate? Swap clothes with a pal, Val. Just get yourself free.

A note on being terrible

Look, I am a terrible person. We may as well get that out of the way now. My showers are too long, my Uber journeys are too short. Sometimes I don't rinse out my peanut butter jar for recycling. Occasionally I don't recycle at all – like on holiday or in someone else's house, where tossing a plastic container into the bin feels like a strange and shameful treat (you know it does, don't lie).

I am vegan except for halloumi, and pizza, and puddings and weekends and Christmas. I leave my chargers plugged in. I stopped using my KeepCup when it started tasting of dishwasher. I will probably never switch to natural deodorant. I'm a terrible person just like you're a terrible person, and the person next to you is a terrible person, and nearly all of us, as privileged folk who use and abuse the world's resources on a daily basis to feed our own daft desires, are terrible people in unique and multifarious ways. It is hard to exist as a human in the developed world without sometimes being terrible. Or at least, that's how it feels.

In the pages of this book are a few true saints – people who have dedicated their careers and great chunks of their time and energy to fixing things, fighting wrongs and helping us all to be a little less terrible. But I can guarantee they all feel like terrible people too, at one time or another.

So as long as we're all united in our mutual terribleness, we may as well park that guilt for now. Leave it in the cloak-room so we don't have to lug it round all day. Shall we?

Because you don't get very far with guilt, I find. Not when fast-fashion consumers are predominantly women, and our lives are already so laden with shame. We feel bad about not looking good, bad about trying to look good, and now we feel bad about *being* bad by trying to look good. The odds are stacked against us from the start. 'Just buy less!' isn't a very effective message when everything else is still screaming 'BUY MORE!'

Guilt and shame, while they can be catalysts for change, often use up far too much energy to be helpful. All that stewing over the various ways we've been shitty, and continue to be shitty, selfish, careless, greedy, unethical and unfriendly. It might make us feel temporarily less terrible, but it's also time-consuming and it doesn't get a whole lot done. You catch more flies with honey than vinegar, and you change more with optimism and enthusiasm than you do with self-flagellation.

No, instead of wringing our hands, we can roll up our sleeves and make change. Even just within our own wardrobes. I can't promise there won't be points in this book where we both feel a little terrible. But I can promise that the point is to leave feeling a lot better than we went in.

That used to be how I felt about Zara. These days I'm not so sure.

PART ONE: THE FIGHT

Fashion, we have a problem

IT'S NOT YOU, IT'S THEM.
AND A BIT YOU.

Every breakup has its reasons. You can waste a lot of time trying to apportion blame, dividing the failings and missteps as you might fight over mugs and CDs. Could you both have behaved better? Did one side let the other down? Is it our fault fast fashion became so toxic, and we became so greedy for it?

No! Mostly no. Slightly yes.

It wasn't always like this. Up until as recently as the 1990s, the vast majority of new clothes bought in the UK were made here too. From the Industrial Revolution onwards, textile manufacture was a booming part of the British economy, and in lots of other countries besides.

While it's hard to pinpoint the roots of fast fashion – they stretch back through the post-rationing boom, wartime utility clothing and the earliest tailors mass-producing affordable suits for men – perhaps its most recognisable dawn was the 1960s. The 60s spawned Inditex, which owns

Zara, and Chelsea Girl, now River Island. They saw Paco Rabanne make disposable dresses from paper, and revived dandyism as a youth pastime for men and women alike. And it birthed a fast-fashion icon, at least to anyone who has ever fancied themselves in a floppy hat and poet sleeves: Biba.

The grandmother of today's trendsetters, Biba was born in 1963 as a mail-order company, the brainchild of fashion illustrator Barbara Hulanicki and her husband Stephen Fitz-Simon. Women would send off by post for their cheap, modish dresses, made in limited runs to test popularity and keep demand high.

The brand quickly caught the attention of a fashion editor at the *Daily Mirror*, who ran a sponsored promotion featuring a simple gingham shift dress with matching headscarf, similar to one worn by Brigitte Bardot. Biba hoped to sell around 3,000 dresses. They received over 17,000 orders.[10]

Buoyed by success, Hulanicki and Fitz-Simon opened a boutique in Kensington, which soon became a must-visit for the bright young things of swinging London: 'The most in shop for gear', according to a 1966 issue of *TIME* magazine.[11] Biba's look was alluring – leggy, louche and doll-like, heavily influenced by art nouveau and Pre-Raphaelite paintings – but its genius was its price point. While ready-to-wear trends had previously been the preserve of the wealthy, Biba made cool mass-market fashion affordable to working-class women.

'They were for the girl in the street,' Hulanicki recalled.[12] 'They earned £9 a week and would spend £3 on a bedsitter, £3 on food, and £3 in Biba.'

Part of Biba's early success was also due to celebrity endorsements from the likes of Twiggy and *Ready Steady Go* presenter Cathy McGowan, whose Friday night TV looks were available to buy in-store the very next day. Star style, accessible to everyone. Rings a bell, right? Let's not forget that ASOS was once 'As Seen on Screen', selling halter tops and hipster jeans cribbed off Atomic Kitten.

As Biba's popularity grew so did its stores, eventually expanding into a five-storey Art Deco department store, a decadent, palm-decked pleasuredome that sold everything from fringed lamps and leopard-print négligées to bottles of shampoo and tins of baked beans. Ever democratic, 'Big Biba' was one of the first stores that allowed customers to try makeup on before buying it, and even Hollywood stars could be spotted stripping off in the communal changing rooms (one time, a pregnant Barbara Streisand). The aspiration level was high. The prices, crucially, stayed low.

Possibly too low, as within a year Biba's finances hit the skids and the business was sold to Dorothy Perkins. But the brand had influence far beyond its awning. Any time you've craved suede knee-high boots or a vision-obscuring fringe or admired the style merit of flamingoes, it was probably at least partly down to Biba. More than just clothes, Biba was a cultural moment. And like all great cultural moments, it echoes.

In 2009, Hulanicki designed a collection for Topshop. After the last of my university finals, I pegged it to the store and bought one of her dresses – bright coral with puffed sleeves and a print-like bacteria under a microscope. I wore it and loved it for a few blissful months, until it shrunk in the wash, the crêpe started pulling at the seams, and it was relegated to the recycling pile. Lo, the legend was complete.

As fast fashion has gathered pace over the past five decades, the democratisation of style has been the main point in its favour. Perhaps the only point in its favour, you could argue, but one that definitely can't be ignored. They might thrive online rather than on Kensington High Street, but in many ways Boohoo, Missguided and Pretty Little Thing are Biba reincarnate. Fashion for young women, fun women, skint women, impatient women, women who see no reason they shouldn't be able to dress exactly like their heroes, be they Meghan Markle or Molly-Mae from *Love Island*. Not just women either, and not only the bright young things with time on their hands and beauty on their side. Everyone! Fast fashion is for everyone. That's the promise, so where's the catch?

Over time, fashion has become an outward display of culture and identity woven tight into the fabric of our society, and one in which we're all expected to participate – so it makes sense that we've wanted accessible options, and grabbed them with both hands when they've arrived. 'Fast fashion has allowed all segments of society, irrespective of class, income or background to engage in the hedonistic and psychogenic pleasures of fashion,' Dr Mark Sumner of Leeds University School of Design told the government's Environmental Audit Committee.[13] 'At no other time in human history has fashion been so accessible to so many people across our society.'

Our society. There's the catch.

Because while fast fashion here may have been a great leveller, at least as far as income is concerned, elsewhere it's having a starkly different effect.

These days only a tiny fraction of our clothes are made in Britain, with the vast bulk of garment production offshored – mainly to developing nations such as China, Indonesia, India and Bangladesh, where labour is cheap, hours are brutal and workers have little power to resist. As shoppers carry on chasing the best bargains around the internet, the fashion industry carries on 'chasing the cheapest needle' around the world. On it goes and faster it gets, until it's virtually impossible to extricate supply from demand. We keep buying it, so they keep making it. They keep making it, so we keep buying it. It's hard to see exactly where most blame lies, but one thing is clear: someone needs to be first to slam on the brakes.

While Biba customers frolicked in their hip Victoriana (see, fashion has always been a rehash!), their parents and grandparents, actual Victorians, were probably bewildered. Back then, a new outfit represented an investment of time as well as money. Hours spent, weeks waited, hems and seams altered over the years as fashion changed, or you did.

Not so much now. Now, we use 'shop' as a verb almost entirely detached from its results. 'In case you fancy a shop!' is the message that gets sent round those email chains of Black Friday discount codes. Or did, until it became cooler to talk loudly about how you'll be in your underground bunker thinking about capitalism.

And when it comes to shopping, it's easy to slip into another modern habit – the one where we reframe our behaviour as noble and good and actually fine, fiiiiiine – rather than being arsed to stop doing it. Treating ourselves to something pretty can be nattily repackaged as self-care. 'Being kind to ourselves'. Why should we change our behaviour, we might ask, when life is so hard and clothes are so nice, and anyway it's the industry that's to blame?

Well, it's a fair point. While deep down we know that there's probably more to self-love than sinking further into your overdraft with yet another wrap dress, hauling ourselves over the coals doesn't achieve much either. (Please see: terrible).

'There's being informed, and then there's self-flagellation. It's always a really fine balance between the two,' agrees Sophie Slater, co-founder of ethical feminist fashion label Birdsong and one of my favourite voices of reason in the industry. Like many of the sustainable fashion advocates I've spoken to in this book, she believes there's too much burden placed on consumers, and not nearly enough on the fashion industry or the bodies that should be regulating it.

'They're making, what, eight billion garments a year? And that's more than we could ever wear,' she says. 'It's about big companies churning out literally billions of items of clothing and then spending billions of pounds making you want them.'

It's a system that fails consumers too. 'Fast fashion brands rip off people on lower incomes, because they don't deliver decent products,' adds Slater. 'You have to buy them again and again and again. It's not the consumer's fault at all, nobody should be shamed – we all do what we feel we need to do to survive.'

We can only do the best we can do.

Of course, the fashion chains could argue the same thing. They're doing what they need to do to survive in a retail landscape where everyone's too scared to take their foot off the pedal. When you consider that retailers like Zara can get a garment from the drawing board to the shop floor in as little as ten days, it's hardly surprising some of the clothes aren't worthy of a longer lifespan.[14] If designers and manufacturers had a little longer to mull things over, do you think we'd have seen The Summer of the Cold Shoulder Top circa 2014? Really?

Or, if we're feeling generous to the fashion brands, we could go a step higher and blame our neoliberal, market-driven government. After all, our shopping habits are driven by another unlikely influencer: the Chancellor of the Exchequer. Successive chancellors may not know how to style a slip dress, but they are keen to keep us buying them, along with anything else that brings in precious tax revenue. When we read about the 'death' of the British high street, it's often laced with blame – as though it's our public duty to shop till we drop, lest the economy does instead.

By this point the argument begins to feel like the giant tangled pile of tights in my second drawer. Its many flailing strands almost impossible to separate out. Each one flimsy, many opaque, plenty full of holes. We could stay at this stalemate forever, passing the buck from ourselves to the brands to the government and back, and all the time those eight billion garments would still be flying off the benches of underpaid workers, to be underutilised, underappreciated, and ultimately buried underground.

So perhaps instead of asking who is to blame, what we need to ask instead is: who can make the biggest difference? The surprising answer is, it might be us.

'I personally think the group that is most likely to make a change is consumers,' says Dr Sumner, when I call him to try and sort out the tangled tights pile.

'They make decisions. They're the ones that ultimately say: "I'm going to buy that." But the group that it's most difficult to engage with, to change, is also consumers. It's a double-edged sword.'

It's the same message I get from Neliana Fuenmayor, founder of A Transparent Company, a creative intelligence network which helps fashion businesses practise greater transparency. 'Every day, we vote with our wallets,' she says. 'As consumers we have the right to ask and demand answers. That is how the brands will accelerate and change. If the consumer stays passive, so the brands will too.'

And it's echoed by Stella McCartney in the 2015 pioneering documentary film *The True Cost*. 'The customer has to know that they're in charge. Without them, we don't have jobs,' she says. 'If you don't like it, you don't have to buy into it.'[15]

The truth is, fashion needs us more than we need fashion. Without thousands of thirsty shoppers emptying their racks every week, companies will be forced to take stock and do things differently. But maybe we're so used to feeling enslaved to the high street that we've lost sight of our own clout as consumers. While we still believe that fashion has the power to validate us, fix us, comfort us and complete us, it's hard to feel as though we hold any cards at all. Besides Visa.

That feeling has been drummed into us for most of our lives, by an economy that relies on us believing that too much is never enough. When you've grown up in a world that tells you you're only as good as your last outfit, the belief runs many layers deep. We can't just flip a switch and turn it off, but we can unpick it and examine it. We can clear out a few of those emotions, along with our wardrobes.

Once you believe that we actually have the collective potential to slow down fast fashion, it makes the break-up feel less like a miserable sacrifice and more like a positive thing. A power move. We might have done nothing wrong, but it doesn't mean we can't try to do things right. We can only do the best we can do, *but most of us can probably do better than we are.*

We can think a little more, and buy a lot less. We can acknowledge the part we play in feeding the monster, however small and inconsequential it might seem in the vast, messy scheme of things. And we can learn. We can listen. We can fight that impulse (entirely natural, I think) to stick our fingers in our ears and lalalala the facts away.

Because once we understand *why* we're doing this, it makes the doing easier. So here goes.

*'There is no beauty in the finest cloth if it makes
hunger and unhappiness.'*

– Kasturba Gandhi, *Gandhi*[16]

WHERE'S THE HUMANITY?

Let's start by doing what fast fashion so often doesn't. Putting the people first.

It can be easy to see fast fashion as a blank canvas. Soulless, brand-new, squeaky-clean clothes, divested of story or meaning until the moment we pick them up and take them home.

But of course they're not – all those clothes have a tale to tell, every top and skirt and pair of jeans swinging from a high-street rail, every pleather bag and pair of discount shoes orphaned in the dregs of the online sale section. They each have a story already sewn into their seams, often epic in scale, covering thousands of miles and filled with human voices. But it's a story we tend not to think about, and they're voices we choose not to hear. Because we don't know where they are, or we don't have the emotional bandwidth. Because it's just a basic top on a rail.

We know about sweatshops, perhaps. Vaguely. Their spectre has haunted the high street for a while now, as have shadowy ideas of child labour and modern slavery. Sometimes there are faces attached, occasionally a name in a news report, but more often they're reduced to a grimly satirical punchline. Those cheap trainers or that heavily embellished dress were 'probably made by an eight-year old', we quip. And then we grimace. And then we buy them.

But the reality of the modern-day garment industry is something that most of us find it hard to get our heads around, and for fair reason. It's huge and unwieldy, full of so many contradictions and complexities that even academics struggle to sum up the best route forward. But that makes sense in itself, because people are full of contradictions and complexities, and people are the force behind fast fashion.

While so much of the modern world has become slickly automated, garment production is still one of the most labour-intensive industries in the world, employing an estimated one in six people alive.[17] Humans are central at every stage of the supply chain, from the cotton farmers growing the fibres to the secondhand traders sifting through vast bundles of our cast-offs on faraway pavements. At one end of the spectrum there are multimillionaire designers, venerated like artists and treated like rock stars. At the other end, armies of skilled people on lightning-quick production lines, paid hardly enough to live and treated barely better than cattle. At every stage, a person and a community profits or suffers.

Perhaps the most depressing thing about the Rana Plaza tragedy was the fact that workers had already pointed out the cracks that were appearing in the building. Factory bosses knew it was unsafe, and yet workers were ordered to come into work as normal or risk having their wages docked for the month. So they did.

It was a gross disregard for workers' safety, but it was also a symptom of the impossible demand on manufacturers to keep churning out product; the downward pressure of the market illustrated all too literally. The bottom of the supply chain was squeezed and squeezed until it reached breaking point, taking 1,138 people with it.

Rana Plaza was no anomaly. The year before, 250 garment workers had died when the Ali Enterprises factory in Karachi, Pakistan, burst into flames. Two months after that, 117 perished in a fire at the Tazreen Fashion factory in Dhaka. In 2010, twenty-nine people lost their lives in a fire at a nearby sportswear factory, which prompted riots on the streets and clashes with armed police. Less than six months after Rana Plaza fell, another fire killed at least ten people in a nearby knitwear factory. And back in 1911, the Triangle Shirtwaist Factory fire in New York, USA, killed 146 workers. Treacherous sweatshops have existed for centuries – it's just that more recently, they've fallen off our Western radar.

Even with workers earning insultingly little, and many working overtime illegally and forgoing water and toilet breaks, the demand for cheaper and faster production leads to a dismal decline in health and safety. In Cambodia, where up to a million garment workers work across 600 factories for brands such as Gap, H&M and Marks & Spencer,[18] there has been a widespread problem with female garment workers fainting on the job. It's due to the long hours, extreme temperatures and lack of ventilation in factories, although some commentators have suggested there could be an element of mass hysteria too. In November 2016, 360 women collapsed in three days.[19] Each time work grinds to a halt at one of these factories, it can cost hundreds of thousands of pounds in lost productivity. There's no time to be sick, and no time to stop.

Which means there's certainly no time for civil disobedience. Over 90 per cent of workers in the garment industry have no possibility of negotiating their wages and conditions,[20] and those who try to unionise are often threatened with harsh penalties, intimidation, abuse and violence. In 2014, three Cambodian garment workers were shot dead by police during protests for a higher national minimum wage. Problems have rumbled on, with 1,200 workers fired from their jobs after striking in January 2019. Three months later they were reinstated, but the 7,500 workers who lost their jobs after similar strikes in Bangladesh were even less lucky.

Fashion is also the second highest product category at risk of modern slavery (after computers and mobile phones, though that's a whole other panic).[21] But while horror stories can make us sit up and pay attention, do things need to get as bad as *actual slavery* to jolt us into action?

One of the most affecting moments of *The True Cost* is twenty-three-year-old Bangladeshi garment worker and union president Shima Akhter discussing consumer attitudes towards the clothes she and her colleagues make all day. 'People have no idea how difficult it is for us to make the clothing. They only buy it and wear it.' She begins to cry. 'I believe these clothes are produced by our blood.'[22] Watching her is enough to end any spurious ideas we might have about sweatshops being desirable work for some people. They might be 'better than other jobs', or no job, sure. But that's a shamefully low bar.

Looking for the root cause of all this injustice, we end up back in the stalemate of blame. Factory owners feel a crippling pressure to keep on lowering prices or risk losing contracts. The shortfall has to be made up somewhere, and 'somewhere' is generally the place of least resistance: vulnerable workers, who need that business too. Likewise, governments in many of these developing nations are desperate for the economy that big brands bring in, so they keep the national minimum wage low, sometimes less than 20 per cent of a realistic living wage, out of fear that companies will relocate if they're forced to pay more.[23]

And because the brands themselves don't actually own any factories or pay workers directly, they often manage to wash their hands of responsibility. 'We didn't know,' comes the response every time some terrible truth is revealed about pay or conditions – or worse, fatalities. Every time the official statement reads like a PR-scripted shrug. Honest, guv. We had no idea.

But the real question isn't whether they knew; it's why they didn't.

Supply chains are a murky business. It's common practice for factories to take on much larger orders than they could ever manage, and subcontract the work to other factories – often unaudited factories – while companies turn a blind eye. Which is how their labels end up appearing in the rubble. After Rana Plaza it was the brands whose clothes had been found in the building that came under fire, but the truth was it could so easily have been any mainstream fashion retailer. Anything we might be wearing right now.

Right now, since you ask, I'm wearing a white shirt with giant, puffy balloon sleeves. It's vintage, which means the stories it tends to spark in my mind are those of its past owners. Who were they? What did they wear it with? Where did they live, and who did they love? I can spend ages in these flights of fictional nostalgia, imagining the groovy past life my shirt might have lived before I snagged it in the attic of a Hackney antiques shop.

But my shirt is also 100 per cent cotton. Which means at some point in time, a farmer grew and harvested the crops my ludicrous sleeves were made from. Someone else spun it into yarn, and someone else embroidered the floral motif on the front. Who were *they*?, I should ask. How much did they earn from it? Where did they live, and who did they love?

Most of us won't see a cotton shirt and think of India, where the industry has been so overwhelmed by genetically modified seeds and expensive pesticides, while export prices fall, that it has led to a debilitating cycle of debt for thousands of farmers. We won't ruminate on the fact that the past two decades have seen the largest recorded 'wave' of suicides in history, with 296,438 Indian farmers taking their own lives between 1995 and 2015[24] – and the fact that debt is frequently cited as a reason. I certainly didn't.

Most of us won't see a vibrant print and think about dye run-off creating skin conditions and neurological problems for children who live along the Citarum River in Indonesia. Or the 40,000 fingers lost annually by industrial workers in China's Pearl River Delta region.[25] We shouldn't have to, obviously, because none of that should even be happening. But while it is, we can at least take the sheen off those shiny new clothes on the shop floor, each time we find ourselves boggling at a bargain price tag, by asking one basic question: where's the humanity?

While stats play their part in engaging our brains, it's individual stories that get us in the heart. In a 2015 stunt by Fashion Revolution, a vending machine selling T-shirts for €2 was placed in a busy Berlin square.[26] Passers-by would insert the money, but before their T-shirt was dispensed they were shown a video of a garment maker at work in Bangladesh.

'Meet Manisha. One of millions making cheap clothing for as little as 13 cents an hour,' it read, then asked if the person still wanted to buy the T-shirt, or donate the €2 instead.

Nine out of ten people chose to donate. 'People care when they know,' concluded the video.

A cynic might say that people only care because they think others are watching. But a different cynic might say that hardly matters, as long as the results are the same. If we all existed in a vacuum then maybe we'd be pure-hearted models of virtue, or maybe we'd be morally bankrupt arseholes – we don't need to know. Because we're part of a society, and every decision we make has a knock-on impact. An embellished butterfly top beats its wings in a suburban shopping centre and sets into action a chain of events that could last years, and impact thousands.

These days, empowerment now sells the way sex once did. The word 'feminist' appears on retailer homepages and newsletters 6.3 times more often now than it did three years ago.[27] And yet, as 80 per cent of workers in the global garment industry are women aged 18–35,[28] it's young women who suffer for those sassy slogan tees.[29] Nearly one in three garment workers in Cambodia experiences sexual harassment,[30] while studies of garment workers in other developing countries such as Myanmar, Sri Lanka, Vietnam and Indonesia paint a similarly grim picture of abuse and sexual violence. Excessive overtime means that women often have to travel on public buses or walk home late at night too, which many feel unsafe doing alone. Hell, I feel unsafe doing that alone in London. It's the time-old trade-off: female autonomy comes at a price, and often that price is a key between your knuckles.

If we're going to start thinking about the exploitation and inequality tied up in our seams, then we need to look at the whole picture. Beyond the sweatshops and cotton fields. Where's the humanity on our high street, and in our magazine pages? How does it look, and who's represented?

We need to look at the racism still rife across the industry, and the colonisation and cultural appropriation that has pillaged thanklessly from people of colour for centuries. Not just in advertising and magazine editorial but in the clothes themselves, in prints or collections called 'ethnic', 'tribal', 'Navajo' or any number of words lazily co-opted by designers and marketers without giving any credit (or money) to their human sources of inspiration.

We need to look to the narrow definitions of 'fashionable' beauty that have shaped the way generations of women feel about their bodies. Only 0.69 per cent of A/W 2019's catwalks featured a plus-size model, and only 0.49 per cent featured a woman over fifty.[31] Where's the humanity in that? Or the business sense, for that matter? Sustainable style can't only be about who's behind the sewing machine; it has to be about who has a seat at the table.

That's the manifesto of Aja Barber, a writer, speaker, Instagrammer and fashion consultant who specialises in ethics and inclusivity. For her, one can't exist without the other. 'Think about it this way: the only way the formula can really move as fast as it's currently going is if there's a level of exploitation somewhere,' she says. In the world of Insta-activists hoping to help us all shop 'better' in £300 dresses, Barber is a breath of fresh air and an invaluable voice, reminding her followers that checking supply chains and eco-credentials isn't enough. We need to be checking our privilege, too.

'The first thing we need to do is start looking out for each other,' she continues. 'If your feminism is truly intersectional then you should care what the lady in Bangladesh is being paid to make your "feminism" T-shirt. You should care that workers can support their families and that big businesses which make billions of dollars a year are actually paying their fair share to everyone involved. You should also care that there is affordable clothing for all levels of income, so that families can dress themselves without hassle. You should care that someone who is bigger than you can buy clothing which makes them happy and feel included.'

We should care. It's a long and intimidating tick list, but it makes a hell of an efficient way to filter down our shopping options.

Dr Sumner has been reading up on evolutionary psychology, in an effort to understand how best to get people to change their habits. Human beings, he tells me, don't have a great capacity for thinking about things behind our immediate family and community. 'As a species, we're quite selfish,' he says. 'But to be sustainable, we need to be selfless. And that is a really big challenge.'

I want to believe we're up to the challenge. After all, ours is a sociable age. If the internet has achieved anything, it is getting us to care passionately about things that happen thousands of miles away from us, to people we've never met. Stories can travel faster than the speed of light now, and be amplified across continents. If we give it a chance, that connectivity could sound a death knell for fast fashion as it stands. We can find out what we need to know.

And people care when they know.

'In nature's economy the currency is not money, it is life.'

– Vandana Shiva[32]

NO PLANET B

The planet is so hot right now. You'd have to be living in a hole in the ground not to be aware of the threat of climate change – and from the sounds of it we might all end up in one, if things don't improve. Fast.

As I write this, the UK Parliament has become the first in the world to declare an environment and climate emergency, setting the target for net zero carbon emissions by 2050. It's progress, but the mood is sceptical. The mood is always sceptical. Will it change anything? After all, you can understand you're in the middle of a disaster and still carry on fanning the flames. We can all be the internet's favourite dog meme, drinking a cup of coffee in a burning room and telling ourselves everything's fine.

'Our house is on fire,' began sixteen-year-old Swedish activist Greta Thunberg's speech to Davos in early 2019. 'I am here to say, our house is on fire.'[33]

By 2040, we could be in the midst of a planetary catastrophe. Rising sea levels will engulf coastlines, droughts will intensify, food will be scarce and the coral reefs will be gone. We have eleven years, says the Intergovernmental Panel on Climate Change, to cut CO_2 emissions by 50 per cent and keep global warming to a maximum of 1.5 degrees, or it could be be too late to undo our mistakes.[34] Some say the reality is less than that. Some say we're already living on borrowed time.

You might say: what's this got to do with what I'm wearing?

Unfortunately, quite a lot. Textile production produces an estimated 1.2 billion tonnes of CO_2 equivalent (CO_2e) per year, which is more than international flights and maritime shipping combined.[35] That's before we even get on to the impact of packing, shipping and delivering our clothes, displaying them in stores, promoting them via lavish fashion weeks and press events, or pushing them via the mail-order catalogues that go straight from our doormat to the bin. Before we talk about washing them and dry-cleaning them, and what happens when we throw them away. Before we get into the moral question of animal products like leather, silk and wool, or the destruction of habitats that could be losing us whole species for ever.

Fashion may or may not be the world's second biggest polluter, but arguing the point too strenuously feels like setting up a deckchair on the wrong side of history. Whether it's second, third or sixth, the fact stands that there are huge environmental problems at both ends of the fashion food chain. Textile waste is a growing problem with a scarily uncertain outcome, while textile production is a greedy beast, guzzling resources on a mind-blowing scale and stunting the very communities it claims to develop.

Yet fashion is a bit of a surprise in the climate change conversation. We've known for a while now that we need to cut down on fossil fuels, avoid plastic, drive less, fly less, eat local, eat vegan, quit quinoa and carry a canvas tote bag, but the idea that our clothes could be destroying the planet, both before we buy them *and* after we get bored of them, has been new information to process. We care when we know, but most of us simply didn't.

For lots of people the wake-up call came in late 2018, when the BBC aired *Stacey Dooley Investigates: Fashion's Dirty Secrets*. While Dooley's brand of activism has at times proved controversial, her ability to reach a mainstream audience is undeniable. The show was an hour full of shocks and revelations, not least around a fabric that has long been on the 'nice' list: cotton.

To many of us, cotton still represents a kind of purity. It has a rep as the moral opposite of synthetic fibres; the all-natural angel to plastic's sweaty devil. But the reality is more complicated (when is it ever not?).

While it's true that cotton is breathable, grows naturally and biodegrades, it also uses more pesticides than any other crop in the world. These spread to waterways and harm animal life, while insects build up resistance, forcing cotton farmers to use more and more chemicals and spend more and more on new formulations. Cotton is also the planet's thirstiest crop, using about 2,700 litres of water to grow enough to make a single T-shirt.[36] Which is a huge figure, although hard for the average shopper to put into any kind of context – until we're told that it's enough for one person to drink for 900 days. One of the 1.1 billion people worldwide who don't have access to fresh water perhaps.[37] Or until we're shown the cotton-growing regions of Kazakhstan and Uzbekistan, where so much water has been diverted from waterways to irrigate cotton fields that the fourth-largest lake in the world has almost vanished. Gone.

Stats and stories have their place, but sometimes it takes visuals to grab our attention. This was one of those moments: Dooley standing in the middle of the desert formerly known as the Aral Sea, trying to wrap her head around the fact that a body of water nearly the size of Ireland has disappeared in just over four decades. 'There used to be fish – tens of thousands of tonnes of fish. And now there's a camel.'[38]

The drive across the barren landscape was juxtaposed with footage of the Aral in the 1960s, of happy family boat trips on its twinkling turquoise waters. But the tragedy of the story is not just the loss of a natural beauty spot – it's the poisonous dust storms, filled with leftover pesticides, which now engulf the area. Tuberculosis, stroke and cancer rates have all risen among local people, partly as a direct result of the carcinogenic dust, but also due to plummeting quality of life in the region's fishing communities. As the water dried up, so did the incomes that depended on it. But the cotton kept growing, and the clothes kept coming.

I've strayed back into talking about human problems now, but that's inevitable. Fashion's environmental issues are inherently social issues too, because people are always affected – usually the youngest, poorest or most vulnerable first. Delve into any one of fashion's ecological crimes, and sooner or later, you'll find human suffering.

In 2012, an estimated 12.6 million people died as a result of living or working in an unhealthy environment.[39] And, at a time when we use the word 'toxic' to describe masculinity, melodramatic friendships or Britney's finest legacy, there are millions of people living with very real toxicity in their lives. Many of them are in the textile-producing regions of China, India and Indonesia, who drink water polluted by untreated chemicals dumped into rivers by nearby factories. A 2017 report found that parts of India's Chambal River now run 'dark black water with streaks of red and an intense smell of rotting radishes', thanks to carbon disulphide, a chemical routinely used in the production of viscose.[40] Viscose waste has been linked to the death of fish and aquatic life, as well as myriad health problems including skin burns, Parkinson's, heart attack, stroke, cancer and birth defects.

This might be shocking to us, but it isn't new information. In the early 20th century, viscose was made widely in the UK, US, France, Germany and Russia. But when research began to reveal the risks involved, production was gradually offloaded to Asian countries where labour was cheaper and environmental regulations were lax. This is just one of thousands of examples of westerners exporting our problems to developing nations, rather than trying to solve them.

The good news is, it's possible to make viscose in a much kinder, more sustainable way. The result, lyocell (branded as TENCEL™) is currently the darling of the ethical fashion world, while ancient fibres like linen and hemp are also getting a chic makeover in an attempt to wean us all off synthetics. And there's been a big push towards organic cotton, produced without the toxic pesticides or GM seeds. The Global Organic Textile Standard (GOTS) is the world's leading standard for fabric, guaranteeing that a product with their stamp of approval contains at least 70 per cent organic natural fibres, features no heavy metals, toxic dyes, pesticides or PVC, and has been made to a stringent list of human rights criteria. It's one of a bunch of certifications we can look out for on clothes and shoes to give us a little reassurance.

But the problem isn't just what we wear. It's what we don't.

As our high streets and wardrobes have been flooded with a deluge of cheap fashion over the past twenty years, so the ground has been flooded with its aftermath. Clothes in landfill can take as long as two hundred years to decompose, with synthetic fabrics like polyester still leaching plastic microfibres into the environment long after they're dead and buried. God, think how many different incarnations of boho we could have in two hundred years. Each with its own slightly different wafty 'must-have'.

Our best hope is to move from our linear model (buy > use > dispose > the end) to a circular economy, feeding our cast-offs back into the system to be reborn as something new. Even if clothes look knackered and unwearable to us, there is always a better place for them than the bin.

Clothes recycling is an answer, but it's far from perfect. Regenerating old fibres into new fabric is complicated, labour-intensive and not always worth the energy it uses up – particularly as modern fabric blends are much harder to separate out than 100 per cent cotton or 100 per cent polyester. In an effort to 'close the loop', many high-street retailers now offer take-back schemes, where shoppers can bring unwanted clothes into store in exchange for discounts or vouchers. H&M, & Other Stories, Marks & Spencer, Primark, Zara and John Lewis all have their own versions, but it's doubtful this will ever be able to offset their own damage. In 2013, journalist Lucy Siegle worked out that it would take H&M 12 years to recycle 1,000 tonnes of clothing. That's about the same volume it churns out in 48 hours.[41]

The best solution is to keep our clothes in action, whether that's by us or by a brand-new owner.

The average lifespan of a garment varies wildly depending what you read, from 2.2 years[42] to, as one blog I saw the other day blithely declared, five weeks. Some figures focus on the clothes we get rid of, which are most likely to end up festering in landfill or joining the bloated pass-the-parcel of global secondhand clothes trade, but others take into account the clothes that are still in our lives, unworn and unloved. Reportedly 33 per cent of women now consider clothes 'old' after wearing them three times.[43] Those clothes might not be doing any direct harm to the planet, yet, but they still have a knock-on effect – because the less we wear them, the more likely we are to buy more.

As the CEO of clothes waste charity TRAID, Maria Chenoweth is a woman on a mission to emancipate these unworn clothes. In 2018 the charity launched its 23% Campaign in London, sparked by the discovery that 23 per cent of the capital's clothes – that's a colossal 123 million items – were languishing at the back of wardrobes. It sparked a marketing drive, asking people to donate that 23 per cent to TRAID.[44] Within six months the charity had received 221 tonnes of wearable clothes, putting three quarters of a million garments back into circulation and saving an estimated 2,100 tonnes of carbon and 353,600,000 litres of water.[45]

It's an impressive result, but it's only a drop in the ocean. I ask Chenoweth how she thinks we got to this point, where clothes have become disposable and fast fashion a 'monster' – her words – that we just keep on feeding. She wastes no time in laying the blame on capitalism, not consumers. 'The corporation somehow saw an opportunity to make more money and went for it. Big time.'

As her weapon to slay the monster, Chenoweth has TRAID's network of more than 1,500 charity clothes banks nationwide, which divert 3,000 tonnes of clothes waste from landfill every year and raise funds for international textile industry development projects via eleven charity shops and an eBay store. She also has a philosophy. 'People need to start being kind. And this kindness should be from ourselves and how we consume, but it should also be from the buyers, the suppliers, the shareholders ... we just need to be kind and thoughtful. Instead of, "I don't care, I'm just going to trample on these people to make this organisation more profit,"' she says. 'Who ARE the people making all this money? Who ARE they?'

As well as an unwitting Nikki Grahame impersonation, it's a salient point: we should be tracing our supply chains up as well as down, to know exactly whose pocket we're lining. If thinking about fast fashion's victims doesn't quite do the trick, then picturing Philip Green's grinning face every time we're about to drop a wad in Topshop might.

Ultimately, money is driving the juggernaut. Whether it's textile tycoons and chemical manufacturers making millions, or us saving a few quid on a sweatshirt, the greenest thing about fast fashion as it currently stands is the dollars it generates. It isn't too late to turn things around, but we're going to need progress that whirrs even faster than the production line.

'I think, well, should I have had children? What's it going to look like for them?' says Chenoweth.

The question of what will happen if nothing changes is a shadowy one, often asked in climate change conversations but rarely answered with any certainty. Most of us don't know, and if anyone does know, we'd probably rather they didn't say.

But do we even have to know? Isn't the devastation that fast fashion is causing people *right now* enough reason to change our shopping habits? As US environmentalist Gus Speth wrote in 2010, 'All that human societies have to do to destroy the planet's climate and biota and leave a ruined world to future generations is to keep doing exactly what is being done today.'[46]

A decade on from that statement, we'd better hope our style is changing. Because in another ten years' time, we need things to look very different indeed.

10 stats to pay attention to

To be read and recited during difficult moments, such as condescending dinner party conversations, or when you blink and find you're magically in House of Fraser.

1. Textile production produces an estimated 1.2 billion tonnes of CO_2e per year, which is more than international flights and maritime shipping combined.[47]

2. The average person buys 60 per cent more items of clothing than they did just fifteen years ago, and keeps them for about half as long.[48]

3. By 2030, global clothing consumption is projected to rise by 63 per cent, from 62 million tonnes to 102 million tonnes. That's equivalent to more than 500 billion extra T-shirts.[49]

4. By 2050, the equivalent of almost three earths could be required to provide the natural resources it would take to sustain our current lifestyles.[50]

5. A polyester shirt has more than double the carbon footprint of a cotton shirt.[51] And yet the cotton needed to make a single T-shirt can take 2,700 litres of water to grow – that's enough drinking water to last a person three years.[52]

6. At its current rate, the fashion industry is projected to use 35 per cent more land to grow fibres by 2030. That's an extra 115 million hectares of land that could otherwise be used to grow food, or left to protect biodiversity.[53]

7. Approximately 80 per cent of workers in the global garment industry are women aged 18–35.[54] But only 12.5 per cent of clothing companies have a female CEO.[55]

8. Among seventy-one leading retailers in the UK, 77 per cent believe there is a likelihood of modern slavery (forced labour) occurring at some stage in their supply chains.[56]

9. More than 90 per cent of workers in the global garment industry have no possibility of negotiating their wages and conditions.[57]

10. Increasing the price of a garment in the shop by 1 per cent could be enough to pay the workers who made it a living wage.[58]

> 'If I buy cheap clothes, I just see the faces of the sweatshop workers. And if I buy expensive clothes, I just see all of the faces of the people in poor countries who would eat for a year on that money. So I can only really be happy naked.'
>
> – Deborah Frances-White[59]

CHEAP AT TWICE THE PRICE

When my mother was a teenager in the early 1970s, she had a Saturday job in a jewellery shop. She earned £5 a week, which was a pretty decent wage for her age at the time.

As she remembers it, a day dress from a high street shop like Chelsea Girl would typically cost £16.99. Almost a month's wages. Three and a half Saturdays of helping hapless men choose bracelets for their wives, worrying about the threat of armed robbery and fending off casual groping commensurate with the decade, to buy a single dress.

By comparison, three decades later, my teenage Saturday job in a local library earned me about £50 a week. And I could still buy a dress for £16.99.

You probably know from your own versions of these anecdotes that clothes have been getting cheaper for a long time now. While so many other everyday price tags have inflated to an all-time high (ask a baby boomer what they paid for their first home and try not to gnaw your fist like it's an underripe avocado), fashion has done the opposite; the snowballing effect of cheap labour, industry competition and customer expectation has sent prices plummeting. Just as Ernie Elmo Thingy predicted, clothes have crossed over from investment pieces to near-disposable items, with price tags to match.

Even on a mass scale, it's pretty much impossible to manufacture clothes at toothpaste prices without cutting some serious ethical corners. Garment workers will typically earn 1–3 per cent of the retail price of an item of clothing, meaning that if a T-shirt costs £8, the worker who made it would receive 24p at most.[60] To double the worker's wage would only cost us, the consumers, another 24p. That's pocket change most of us would surely be happy to cough up, if the high street gave us the option. Which is easy to say, because it doesn't.

So, we might conclude: cheap is bad. Got it. Must spend more!

But nothing is that simple. For starters, some of us can't spend more. While the stereotype might brand fast-fashion fans mindless consumers, many of us are perfectly conscious. Budget conscious. Living on a low income, as some 14.3 million people in the UK currently do, can make you painfully aware of every single penny going out.[61] It means constantly doing the mental trade-off: new clothes vs rent, vs food, vs transport, vs health, vs freedom, vs life-long debt.

In a society where the odds are increasingly stacked against anyone from a less privileged background, fast fashion has been a small leveller. It might be fuelling the idea that we need a new outfit every Friday night, but it also clothes kids who wouldn't otherwise have a new pair of school trousers, and the parents who work two jobs to give them that. It helps skint teens feel less conspicuous alongside show-off classmates. It allows struggling pensioners to buy gifts for their families. It isn't a private education, a fancy holiday or a mortgage, but it's a way to participate. To ignore all that and brand every fast-fashion shopper as a stupid capitalist stooge would be massively missing the point.

But at the same time, when we praise cheap clothes as a boon for less affluent people, we only mean the people within our immediate view. If we zoom out and take in the wider pic-ture, the poorest people on the planet are overwhelmingly the ones being hurt by fast fashion – not the ones enjoying it.

Beyond unarguable poverty, there are so many other rea-sons shoppers shop cheap. There's arguable poverty: the less-desperate everyday skintness that sends so many of us through Primark's doors at one time or another. Being a student, a recent grad, a new parent, a person whose boiler has just broken on the same day they had to pay their tax bill. Wealth is subjective, and you don't have to be living on the breadline to feel that cheapest clothes are your most sensible option.

Even when we could perhaps afford to spend a little more, there's the lingering feeling that splashing cash on clothes is a reckless indulgence – especially when there are other things to save for, like future houses, future children and future root canals. There are the voices of a million purse-lipped mothers in our heads ('ONE HUNDRED POUNDS? And it's not even lined!') putting us off too. When we've had it drummed into us that spending big on individual purchases is a sin or a sign of stupidity, it's hard to reprogramme that mindset.

And so, somewhere along the way, buying cheap became a noble thing. A badge of honour. There's a reason that yelling 'THANKS, PEACOCKS!' or wherever has become a state-ment as relatable and meme-able as 'THANKS, IT HAS POCKETS!' While 'shit' trainers and charity-shop clothes have long held a stigma for those who can't afford anything else, those who *can* afford more are supposed to spend less out of humility.

Celebs who wear high-street clothes get applauded for their down-to-earth credentials, for kindly throwing us mortals a bone. I have a very specific and fairly embarrassing memory from when I was about thirteen, after a shopping exped-ition. Alone in front of my bedroom mirror, I mimed walking down the red carpet at a film premiere in my new outfit (button-down corduroy miniskirt, off-the-shoulder prairie top – very Emma Bunton in the 'What Took You So Long?' video). 'Who are you wearing?' the imaginary paps shouted at me. 'Primark!' I called back. That was the kind of star I wanted to be when I grew up. The kind who keeps it real. Jenny from the cul-de-sac.

But then, as I've got older, I've found myself moving away from the flimsiest end of fast fashion and towards the clothes that feel *better*. Better made, nicer cuts, softer fabrics, timeless, um . . . fine, expensive. I just mean more expensive. I hit thirty and, despite earning precisely no more money than I did at twenty-six, my perception of what I can 'afford' magically went up by about a third.

You know the brands I mean. They lure you in with good sales and nice candles, and you kid yourself you can afford them because you're a grown-up now. Maybe you *can* afford them, but not if you carry on shopping like you're still at Peacocks. And certainly not if you're going to spend half a month's rent or mortgage on something like a taupe cashmere onesie or a bib-fronted pinstripe artist's smock with no back, never wear it, and cry any time you put it on because you are not That Woman.

If the cheap and cheerful end of the high street is busy appealing to everywoman, then the mid-range stores are focused on making us wish we were That Woman. You know her. Always chooses exactly the right coat for the weather. Wears complicated oversized wrappy things without ever looking like the Dalai Llama. Can leave her hair in a topknot all day and then shake it down without a kink. Casually rustles up three Ottolenghis while doing witty small talk over her shoulder. Has a PhD but doesn't mention it. Great at sex. Never spills. That Woman.

It's so easy to assume that because something costs half a month's rent and comes in a thick cardboard carrier bag with grosgrain handles, it's automatically better. Because the price tag is fastened on with a trusting safety pin rather than plastic, because the store is full of houseplants, but mainly because *the clothes cost more*, we tell ourselves they must be sustainable. I mean, probably, right?

Sadly no. 'The price you pay for the garment is not always reflective of the quality of the garment, and definitely not reflective of the sustainability of the garment,' confirms Dr Sumner.

Anthropologie, no matter how many hippie-luxe dresses and zodiac coasters it stocks, has failed to score above 10 per cent in the Fashion Transparency Index for the past three years.[62] Whistles is rated 'not good enough' in the Good On You directory.[63] Ditto Toast, for all its wholesome homespun charm. Reiss, French Connection, Jigsaw, L.K. Bennett and Boden all score 'very poor' environmental ratings and only two out of five in the people and animal categories. Free People, ironically enough, publishes no supplier details or evidence of paying a living wage. Danish dreamboat Ganni gets a big fat 'avoid', which is handy because my bank balance was doing that for me already.

After the Rana Plaza disaster it was the notorious budget brands like Primark, Zara and Mango that were front and centre in the heat of the media criticism, whether they had proven links with the factories in the building or not. They were the ones forced to make the biggest improvements – or at least public overtures towards change – while fancy brands have largely been able to fly under the radar, cushioned by their premium image.

And it's not like shelling out really big bucks buys you peace of mind either, as the so-called 'fast luxury' market is growing at a worrying clip. A 2018 list of fashion brands not compliant with the requirements of the Modern Slavery Act reads like a Bond Street shopping list.[64] Valentino, Versace, Tory Burch, Diane von Furstenberg, Salvatore Ferragamo, Longchamp, Furla. The 2019 Fashion Transparency Index tells a similar story – Tom Ford slumped at the bottom with a 0 per cent score, while Dolce and Gabbana fared worse than Forever21, and Chanel was rubbing against Matalan.[65] I'm sure they'd love that.

And let's not forget that, in an act of hauteur even Hyacinth Bucket herself might think excessive, Burberry incinerated £28.6 million of unsold stock in 2017 alone.[66] These vanity bonfires aren't uncommon among luxury brands. They'd rather £28.6 million of perfectly good product went up in smoke than see their brand cheapened a cent by discounted sales to the 'wrong' sort of customer.

Even a 'Made in Britain' label isn't the reassurance it's often touted to be. The phrase might conjure images of rolling hills and proud craftspeople sharing cups of tea with Jerusalem playing in the background, but the reality for many UK textile workers is far less cosy. In 2015, an investigation found that the majority of Leicester's 11,700 garment workers were paid below national minimum wage, many working excessive overtime without employment contracts, in conditions well below health and safety standards.[67] Three years later, journalist Sarah O'Connor found that many workers at small Leicester factories were still earning as little as £3.50 per hour. That's less than half the minimum wage.[68] But it's 25p more than the cheapest dress currently listed on Boohoo.com, a brand that proudly sources half of its clothes from British factories.

And all the while, the rich get richer. Oxfam says it takes just four days for a CEO from one of the top five global fashion brands to earn what a Bangladeshi garment worker will earn in her lifetime.[69] In 2009 the village of Linkenholt in Hampshire was bought in its entirety, for £25 million, by Stefan Persson, the billionaire owner of H&M and the richest man in Sweden. Even bucolic English life can now be sponsored by mass-market fashion.

So, you might ask, if a village costs £25 million ... how much should we spend on a pair of jeans? It's a GCSE maths question for the ages.

Truth is, everyone has their own financial sweet spot; a price tag that represents an emotional investment, but not a reckless extravagance. It's a price that varies with context and circumstance, with age, income and mood. We need to stop shopping as though clothes are toothpaste, but equally we need to stop using the phrase 'investment buy' as a blanket excuse to spaff money we don't have on clothes we don't need. We need to establish what 'value' means to us.

Some people say it should sting a little. That the only way to honour an artisan's hard work is to wince as you're punching your pin in. Some will tell you the biggest outlay should be simple basics like T-shirts and bras, while others will say it should be exotic, flamboyant things that make your heart sing. Lots will say stuff like, 'The best value jeans are the jeans you will wear for years!', overlooking the fact we don't *know* which jeans we'll wear for years until we have bought them and worn them. If we knew instinctively, we wouldn't be in this mess. Life happens, bodies change, seams start to pinch in unexpected places. Even with the best intentions, it's hard to get it right.

We could try doing a kind of mental autocorrect, swapping the word 'cheap' for the word 'exploitative' ('Omg it's sooo exploitative.' 'Hundreds of everyday exploitative prices!'). And we can ask: are the 'investment buys' in our wardrobe earning their keep? Have we worn them endlessly, year after year, or a handful of times out of obligation? Do they make us feel happy and comfy and sexy and confident – and glad we spent that extra ££ that could have gone in an ISA?

Or do they make us feel as guilty and queasy as an £8 T-shirt? Do they make us feel like crap for not being That Woman? Well then.

Of course, if That Woman even exists, she probably doesn't feel like That Woman either. She probably feels exactly like us.

ALL WORN OUT

Hello, do you have too many clothes in your life? There's a club for that – it's called 'everybody' and we meet every morning, throwing heaps of rumpled tops round the room and shouting, 'I AM SO LATE IT'S NOT EVEN FUNNY.'

Not to brag, but the full wardrobe meltdown is my signature move. Grunting, screaming. Sweating, usually. Often I am still in my pants, whirling rejected pairs of trousers around my head like a kind of sartorial semaphore, ten minutes after I'm meant to have left the house.

Since quitting fast fashion I have my meltdowns far less frequently, but I'd be lying if I said they'd stopped altogether. There are still those days when the 'wrong' outfit can feel like a public humiliation or a physical itch. The days where all you want is a sign to wear, broadly in the same vein as a 'Baby on Board' badge, that says something like: 'Please don't look at my trousers.'

I know this sounds ridiculous, I do. But I also know that telling myself 'they're only clothes, you twat' doesn't do much to get me out of the door on time. When I'm in the grips of my worst panic – that frantic, heart-pounding, entirely overwhelming sense that everything is doomed – there isn't much separating my wardrobe anxiety from any other kind of anxiety. It's a physiological reaction to a perceived danger; in this case, the danger of making the wrong choice and wearing a bad outfit all day. I know, ridiculous. I know, I know, I know.

The sheer scale of fashion options available to us in the 21st century isn't only a problem for the planet, and for the people making them. It's starting to mess with our heads, too. Abundant choice is one of modern life's biggest privileges, but it can also be a mental burden. 'Cognitive overhead', the thinkpieces call it now. 'Argh, I don't knoooooow', the rest of us call it, as we freeze up while staring at a lunch menu or find ourselves paralysed by indecision in the tights aisle.

As Barry Schwartz put it in his legendary book *The Paradox of Choice: Why More Is Less*: 'When people have no choice, life is almost unbearable. As the number of choices increases . . . the autonomy, control, and liberation this variety brings are powerful and positive. But as the number of choices keeps growing, negative aspects of having a multitude of options begin to appear. As the number of choices grows further, the negatives escalate until we become overloaded. At this point, choice no longer liberates, but debilitates.'[71]

Fittingly, the book opens with an anecdote about buying a pair of jeans.

Too many options, Schwartz teaches, can give us high stress levels, low self-esteem, inflated expectations and impossible-to-meet standards. The more there is to choose from, the more likely we are to compare ourselves negatively to other people and berate ourselves for choosing badly. The more there is out there to own, the less we're satisfied with what we have. And increasingly, we're starting to realise that this is another drawback of fast fashion. 'Decision fatigue'. Having too many bloody clothes.

Too many, yet never enough. Recent research suggests around 14 per cent of adults in developed countries now have a form of compulsive buying, which is classified as a behavioural addiction – and it's on the rise, particularly among young women in low income groups.[72] 'This may well be because at this age, excessive behaviour is often socially acceptable among peers so the condition may go unrecognised for longer,' comments Peter Schofield from Sheffield Hallam University.[73] Acceptable, or even encouraged? I reckon more than 14 per cent of us regularly feel a twinge of what the writer R.T. Naylor termed 'possessive-compulsive disorder': the unshakeable belief that we are what we own.

There is perhaps no better symbol of this consumer overload, in my life at least, than Oxford Street. London's retail heartland, a 1.9 kilometre stretch of pure, unadulterated capitalism that runs like a thick artery through the heart of the West End. It's a road people fly halfway round the world to selfie on. It was on Oxford Street that William Morris opened his first physical store in 1877, selling the same arts and crafts print designs that hipster maisonettes are papered in and furnished with today. 'If you want a golden rule that will fit everything, this is it: Have nothing in your houses that you do not know to be useful or believe to be beautiful,' as goes his most Pinterestable quote.[74] A rule we should probably be applying to our wardrobes.

And it's on Oxford Street that I would end up, somehow, at least three times a week. Without necessarily planning to, certainly without wanting to, but apparently powerless to avoid it. It was like a homing instinct. I'd open my front door intending to go for a walk, black out and regain consciousness three hours later in Mango with an armful of jumpsuits and no memory of how I got there.

Both the best and worst thing about Oxford Street is that the shops stay open until 9pm or 10pm most nights, to cash in on the 'had two negronis with dinner' crowd. And so my most reckless and regrettable purchases were often made through a haze of Campari and a toddler-like resistance to bedtime. Why go home and sleep when you can just stay out and buy things?

Socialising often takes me to the area, as do work meetings and the Victoria line interchange and the perpetual need to buy someone a something from Oliver Bonas. And that easy over-familiarity with one of the world's most visited shopping destinations isn't good for me, any more than, say, eating a full Christmas dinner five times a week would be good for me. We're just not built for that much excitement.

I've had some of my worst consumer meltdowns on Oxford Street, and some of my biggest existential crises. I cannot 'pop' to the shops. Or 'nip', I can't nip either. 'I'll be back in an hour!' I used to text my boyfriend after work, and three hours later he would check Find My Friends to see my little orange dot still pinballing around W1. While a perfect brain would take in a thoroughfare of such scale and say, 'Ah, plenty to go around!', look in three shops and call it a day, mine would see it as a thrown-down gauntlet. I'm a Gladiators contender; Oxford Street is my Travelator. And it breaks me every time.

The strange thing about living in a world of abundance and oversupply is that it makes us more worried about scarcity. What if the stream of pretty things suddenly dries up one day? What if this is the last top that looks nice on me, ever? What if I don't buy this jacket/jumper/necklace/hairclip and the regret somehow eats me alive? Fashion FOMO is all part of the marketing strategy. ASOS has literally used 'Get it, or regret it' as a slogan.

'The existence of multiple alternatives makes it easy for us to imagine alternatives that don't exist – alternatives that combine the attractive features of the ones that do exist,' writes Schwartz in *The Paradox of Choice*.[75] And that's exactly what's happening when we find ourselves fifty-six pages deep into the clearance section. We're imagining perfect alternatives that don't exist. We're setting ourselves up for disappointment – and wasting hours of our lives in the process.

Quitting the high street isn't just a charitable act; it could save us time and money and preserve our ever-fraying mental health. Last year, while the nation was at peak KonMari, I interviewed professional organiser Vicky Silverthorn, founder of You Need A Vicky and author of *Start With Your Sock Drawer: The Simple Guide to Living a Less Cluttered Life*. What I expected to be a chat about the decluttering trend ended up being an eye-opening discussion of consumerism, throwaway culture and its impact on our happiness.

'I think that we're gaining more understanding of the difference between wanting and needing. How often do we go to a shop and buy something that we actually *need*?' she said. 'Honestly, the feeling is *amazing* – when you change your life in a way where you stop buying out of impulse . . . when you take away that entitlement that says because something is pretty and it looks nice then you've got to have it.'

She may as well have been reading from my own mental script, and a thousand others. It's pretty. It looks nice. *I have to have it.*

Then she said something that has stayed with me ever since.

'The way I see it, every single item you own, you are responsible for. Whether it's a tiny thing or a big thing . . . even if it's at the back of a cupboard. It's still this tiny little speck in your brain.'

All those tiny little specks add up. In our brains, in our wardrobes, in our phones, in our lives. The specks of things we have bought, and the millions of other specks out there for us to buy, multiplying daily. It's a wonder we get anything done at all. Retail analyst Richard Hyman estimates that our wardrobes are made up of 10 per cent items we need and 90 per cent items we want.[76] If that's true, think how much room there is to cut back.

Once we've learned to tell the difference between want and need, I think we can go one step further and spot the difference between want and *like*. Sometimes, perhaps, we could look at clothes the way we look at art. 'I like that dress' shouldn't have to translate automatically into 'I want that dress' any more than a visit to the Louvre should mean we feel compelled to leave with the Mona Lisa down our trousers.

It would mean unpicking a lot of social conditioning, sure. But to be able to look at a piece of clothing, like it, appreciate it as a gorgeous object, and not feel that stomach-wrenching desire to *possess* it – that would be a triumph. And the flipside. If something ticks all three boxes: like, want, need, how much more will we love it and appreciate it once it's ours?

When I began my #notnewyear, I steered clear of Oxford Street. Most sensible Londoners do this anyway, because life is too short to spend it being buffeted in the face by a tourist's rucksack, but I knew that walking past all those windows was going to prove too hard. So I faced my FOMO head-on and stopped. Instead I would weave and duck through the adjacent streets of Soho, where fashion is more likely to be vintage, conceptual or found on the body of a person queueing for Tawainese steamed buns. As long as I didn't stray two hundred yards to the north, I'd be safe.

Then, after a few months, I found myself on Oxford Street by accident, on my way to meet a friend. I braced myself for the inevitable pull as I walked past Zara, but something else happened instead: I felt tired even thinking about it. The idea of going into the shop was exhausting. I hovered in the doorway, testing myself, feeling like the only sober person on a Friday night train. And a part of me wanted to go in, sure, but a bigger part of me said, 'Ugh, must we?'

I hadn't missed it. I'd missed the new clothes, but I definitely hadn't missed the process. I hadn't missed feeling hot and dehydrated in the changing room queue, or peering at my pores under the fluorescent lights, or rifling through sales racks with my elbows out, eyeing fellow shoppers like vultures around a carcass. Somewhere along the way, 'physical comfort' and 'dinner' had moved up in my priority ranking, above 'acquiring more button-down sundresses'. I was starting to see 'shopping' as an activity distinct from me going about my life, rather than something that should be squeezed into every gap in the day whenever the opportunity presented itself. Just because I *could* shop, I no longer felt I *must* shop. And that was nice.

If we want evidence that fast fashion could be stressing us out, we only need to ask the people who've already slowed down. Sophie Benson, a freelance writer who specialises in sustainable fashion, tells me: 'Since quitting fast fashion cold turkey, I have more money, I'm less anxious and I feel more at peace with who I am and how I look. Plus I don't waste time scrolling endlessly on ASOS, putting stuff on a wish list and then deleting it two weeks later in favour of something else. So that's more time to hang out with my cat.'

'Time management has been a huge, unexpected benefit,' agrees Instagrammer Jade Doherty, @notbuyingnew. 'It's so easy to see my clothes now and choose an outfit easily. I also have a lot more room in my bedroom.'

More space on your floor or in your calendar might sound like a small comfort in exchange for everything you're giving up, but don't underestimate the difference these things can make to our health and happiness. Take it from a person with a bedroom still regularly covered in clothes, but who can now walk up Oxford Street without twitching. When it comes to taking back control of our lives, our time, our money and our mornings, some of us are so late it's not even funny.

'If a blogger I follow has been on holiday wearing the most amazing looks, I suddenly, irrationally hate my holiday wardrobe.'

– Alex Stedman, *The Frugality*

FOLLOWING THE LEADER

We can't talk about navigating the difference between want and need without talking about the internet.

We may have been addicted to fashion long before we were addicted to our phones, but for many of us it's hard to remember a time before the daily scroll informed our purchasing decisions. I've bought clothes online with one eye still closed, before lifting my head off the pillow. I've bought clothes in hospital waiting rooms, on far-flung beaches, and while staring at a woman wearing the same dress in the street.

By wiggling into narrower and narrower cracks in our day, Instagram can catch us during our most insecure moments, when we're primed and ready for a little retail pick-me-up – it knows it can, because it lowered our mood in the first place. It planted that infernal twinge of discontentment (#want #need) that only shopping can cure. If fashion is 'capitalism's favourite child', as German writer Werner Sombart once put it, then the internet is its favourite grandchild.[77] And boy, does it know how to use pester power.

Unmistakably, social media is one of the biggest factors that has changed millennial and Gen Z shopping habits over the past decade. More than a fifth of online shoppers aged 37 and under now use social networks for shopping inspiration, compared to just 5 per cent of online shoppers over the age of 38. Some 21 per cent of online shoppers have made a direct purchase from social media, while 52 per cent have clicked on an influencer's post, and 31 per cent made a direct purchase from the post.[78]

It's a conversion rate traditional advertising can only dream of – which explains why brands are falling over themselves to turn social media's biggest players into walking, talking adverts. Even tighter regulations around influencer transparency haven't slowed the slew of promo posts; increasingly I find my brain just skims over the hashtags while it looks at the pretty pictures. #Spon, #ad, #presstrip and, of course, #gifted, which I like to sing to the tune of 'Lifted' by the Lighthouse Family. I find it takes the sting out of the jealousy.

Because of course I'm jealous, and not just of the free clothes. I want the clothes, but I also want the wisteria-covered townhouse behind them. I want the body that's in them. I want the golden light and the small dog and the freedom to be twirling on sunny pavements on a Tuesday afternoon instead of sitting hunched over a screen. I want it all, but I can't have it all, so the clothes feels like a reasonable compromise. That's how they get us. *Add to basket*.

But this isn't a clear-cut 'them and us'. Sometimes it's not just winsome strangers that are selling to us; it's friends, and sort-of friends, and the sister of someone we met once at a festival. Instagram is a place where anyone, in theory, can flourish, and that egalitarian allure has the power to make wannabe influencers of us all. You notice it sneaking into your mental checklist of outfit considerations in the morning, along with the weather and how much walking you'll need to do that day. 'Will anyone,' you wonder, 'be taking photos?'

Or at least I do, which is embarrassing to admit. But then I've heard #honesty sells too.

The two-way street of social media means we live in greater proximity to our style heroes than ever before. Once upon a time, kids, we used to have to cross busy streets or yell over the music in a bar to ask people where their clothes were from. It was an effort, it risked awkwardness and we were rewarded for our great bravery with the precious intel. Unless they said, 'Oh, I can't remember,' in which case we hated them for ever.

But now, we believe that precious intel to be our god-given right. Instagram is built on a chummy, peer-to-peer sales model; one in which influencers are obliged to end posts about completely unrelated topics with a list of stockists, because otherwise they'll have three hundred comments asking where the T-shirt with 'Levi's' written across it could possibly be from. It's boring for us, but, I imagine, so much more boring for them.

Grace Victory is a blogger, author, podcaster and YouTuber, with 148,000 Instagram followers to her name. She speaks about mental health and body positivity among other things, but like many influencers she feels the pressure to be continually serving up new outfits. 'Audiences often want to go and buy whatever you're wearing too, and sometimes people get a bit annoyed if you show things that are sold out or no longer available,' she says.

It's that illusion of democracy again; followers have got used to being able to instantly 'click to buy!' the clothes they see on their feeds, to the point where showing off an old outfit could feel oddly like a new kind of elitism. It's the new 'Oh, I can't remember'. We hate it, and Victory understands. 'I know that as a consumer, I also get annoyed when another plus-size blogger wears something and I love it, but can't get my hands on it,' she admits.

But Grace says she couldn't abandon mass-market fashion even if she wanted to. 'I've never shopped from any sustainable fashion brands because they do not cater to my size. I'm a UK 20/22 so my options are limited as it is – most *fast* fashion brands don't go to that size, let alone the sustainable ones.'

For many plus-size style bloggers, fast fashion has been a godsend in recent years, and Instagram a vital community for them to share their finds and celebrate style on their own terms. When women who have been sidelined or ignored by traditional fashion media forever are finally starting to build their own platforms, slating them for dressing unethically feels unfair to the point of prejudice. Like pulling the rug out just as they were finally beginning to get comfortable.

'We are critiqued on pretty much everything, and this is now an extra thing to add to the pile,' says Victory. 'While I agree we should all do our bit, we should be very careful with pointing fingers when nobody's perfect.'

As more of us attempt to detoxify our digital lives and step away from our phones, it's possible that the days of #influence are numbered. But is it too optimistic to hope social media could be a solution too? After all, influencers might have the power to tell us what to wear, but they have cut-through and reach that academics and activists don't – and it's part of their job to reflect the changing world around them.

Someone keenly aware of that responsibility is Alex Stedman, fashion editor and author of the wildly successful blog *The Frugality*, who has 237,000 Instagram followers hanging on her every outfit. 'I must admit I have fallen into a trap in the past of thinking only new clothes garnered likes, engagement and growth,' she says. 'But I have stepped back lately and focused more on what I set out to do with my channels, and it has made a difference to my mental health, my bank balance and, hopefully, the environment.'

As with everything, it's about striking a balance. 'No one wants to feel told off,' says Stedman. 'We need to applaud the trying more.'

There's plenty of trying to applaud these days. One by one, the posts have appeared – wardrobe purges and confessionals, pledges to slow down, re-wear more outfits and become more mindful of their habits. Below each post, a flurry of emoji hand claps and promises to do the same.

Some of it, inevitably, feels hollow. There are influencers who will wax lyrical about sustainability in one post and then shill for a fast-fashion giant in the next. But there are also the surprises, like fitness entrepreneur Grace Beverley, who has a one million-strong Instagram following. Beverley launched her own sustainable athleisurewear label, Tala, in 2019. Made with 92 per cent recycled nylon, reasonably priced and (the right kind of) transparent, Beverley's style of influence might not be for everyone – but her efforts deliver far more than a flimsy fig leaf.

Then there are the armies of secondhand, eco-focused or no-buy Instagrammers out there, gaining traction, creating communities, sharing their #ootd (that's old outfit of the day) and urging us all to #chooseused. People follow them for styling and upcycling inspiration, practical tips and to coo over their best charity-shop finds – proof that you can still build an engaged following without wearing anything your followers can go out and buy.

One is the aforementioned Jade Doherty, who posts as @notbuyingnew. Since quitting the high street and committing to a capsule wardrobe of fewer than thirty items, she's grown a community of more than 23,000 followers and is reaping positive rewards. 'I've benefitted from meeting amazing, talented and interesting people who share the same values as me and are finding different ways to make a difference,' she tells me.

Doherty's grid is all outfit shots, but scrolling through it feels like a slow exhale. The same items feature again and again, in different formations. The same jeans with a different jacket, the same jacket over a dress, the same shoes for five days in a row; each piece of clothing like a series regular that you're excited to see reappear. For fashion nerds, it's a lesson in the alchemical balance of a good outfit. To tuck, or not to tuck? A trainer or a sandal? How to stop your linen jumpsuit getting creased during the day? It might not be the engagement-bait of the conventional influencer outfit parade, but it's so much more #relatable for it. After all, this is how real people really dress. Repetitively. Incrementally. Slightly creased. If we can see it, maybe we'll believe it's okay for us to be it.

Meanwhile, the algorithms are quicker to catch on than we are. Since I quit buying fast fashion, my Instagram adverts have changed with alarming speed. Now they're all premium ethical fashion brands – every day, a new one pops up. They're still full of implausibly flawless women in impossibly golden sunlight cavorting in cornfields, and they still make me feel poor, ugly and dissatisfied. But they do it sustainably, so I guess it's a start.

Should you buy that dress everyone has?

A handy checklist!

1. Would you even like this dress if you'd seen it in a shop and not on thirty-four different women on Instagram?

2. Are the women wearing it on Instagram in a normal, comfortable-looking position, or are they leaning against a painted wall with their foot cocked at an awkward angle?

3. Have you ever seen this dress from the back, and if not is there a reason why?

4. Is it £300?

5. Do you have £300?

6. How will you feel when everyone you see inevitably greets you with, 'Ohhh, you've bought *that* dress!'?
   a) Enthusiasm
   b) Mild annoyance
   c) All-consuming regret

7. Do you have at least three upcoming events that you could theoretically wear it to?

8. Events with other people at them?

9. Have you slightly gone off the dress in the time we've been doing this checklist?

10. Well then.

OUR CHOSEN SKIN

Growing up, I had a dressing-up box. Like the best
dressing-up boxes, it wasn't filled with kid-sized cos-
tumes, but with alien items nobody could quite believe were
ever fashionable, not least the grown-ups they'd originally
belonged to. A purple woollen snood. Long strings of plastic
beads. A grey pleather jacket with puffy blouson sleeves.
Fishnet gloves, a velvet waistcoat, a lavender taffeta brides-
maid's dress. Fabric heavy with anecdotes and powdery
whiffs of Anais Anais. I spent hours waltzing around in
outfits from the dressing-up box – not so much pretending as
practising, I felt, for my future role as 'fabulous lady'. Even
then, clothes were the gateway to the promised land.

By adulthood most of us have left the dressing-up box
behind to chase a different kind of fashion fantasy. The one
in which everything we put on is not so much fabulous as
correct. A wardrobe that works as hard as we do. Day to
night! Boardroom to bar! The 'right' outfit for our bodies,

for our age, for the 'right' place, for the 'right' occasion. Tick-tick-tick, well done, you've passed.

But, like Lorraine Kelly winning her tax-avoidance lawsuit by claiming to be a performer playing the role of 'Lorraine Kelly', getting dressed every day as an adult still involves a certain amount of theatrics. Sometimes we're merely looking to dress for the part of 'semi-competent professional' or 'parent with their shit together', but sometimes we stand in front of our wardrobes with the kind of high-stakes creative brief that makes David Bowie's transition from Halloween Jack to the Thin White Duke look like changing your socks. We don't just want to get dressed, we want to be transformed from the outside in.

Clothes are a way of exerting control in a life where so many things seem beyond our control. They're non-verbal communication, articulating things that we can't say and echoing the things that we can. Clothes bring us together; they help us spot our people in a crowd, and declare ourselves part of a tribe. From drag queens and club kids to religious symbols and slogan tees, style has long been used as an outward expression of our inner lives, especially vital to anyone who feels as though they exist on the fringes of society. There's a reason straight, cis white men aren't the most renowned shopaholics among us. Clothes are social and cultural currency, but they can also be a personal relief fund.

Writer, *Vogue* contributing editor and three-and-a-half-foot disability activist Sinéad Burke told the *Guardian* in

2019: 'I use clothes like armour. If I'm walking down the street in a jumpsuit with caped sleeves and loafers, you probably won't think I'm a lost child who needs help finding their parent. Despite it being seen as an exclusive industry, I see fashion as something that unites us.'[80]

That tricky duality, of fashion as something that both oppresses us and empowers us, is echoed by so many of the people I've spoken to. Sometimes in the same sentence. 'Fashion is intrinsically linked to my identity. Living in a marginalised body means that I am often made to feel like I don't belong and that I should just disappear,' Grace Victory tells me. 'Wearing an outfit that I love makes me feel confident and ready to tackle whatever life throws at me.'

But if clothes are our armour, then they can hang heavy on our shoulders. They can be a powerful tool for busting stereotypes and preconceptions, but they can also serve to reinforce them.

It's true that high fashion applauds eccentricity, those fabulous *doyennes* who'll rock up on the front row looking like a jumble sale with sunglasses on, but below the very upper crust, down where the rest of us live, it's safe to say conformity still rules. And while the CEOs in their luxury trackpants and trainers will tell you modern dress codes are shifting, which they are, it'll be a long old time before we fully let go of the idea that clothes make the person. That's why charities exist to dress unemployed people in smart suits for interviews. And it's why I once changed my outfit three times to go to the corner shop for loo roll.

'I think we need to let go, a little bit, of that "dressing for the part" idea,' says Dr Dion Terrelonge, a chartered psychologist who specialises in fashion and style psychology. She runs a personal styling business with a cognitive wellbeing angle, and as such she has whole case files of evidence that clothes can be a crutch, a comfort, but also a mouthpiece for our inner critic. 'There's a lot of research out there that says, "If you wear a trouser suit to work, you'll be taken more seriously and feel more powerful,"' she says. 'But isn't that because trousers are associated with masculinity, and masculinity is still seen as more powerful?'

We can say we dress for ourselves, not others, but our wardrobes will always reflect social expectations to some extent – because culture seeps into our consciousness without us even knowing it, but also because it's society selling us those clothes in the first place.

Birdsong's Sophie Slater is keen to remind me that we're all victims of a force much bigger than ourselves: marketing departments. 'We are all at the mercy of the industry,' she says. 'It's not your fault that you want it – it's their *job*. They're spending millions and millions of pounds to make you want to buy it.' And, I might add, millions and millions of pounds to routinely shift our attention away from their deficiencies, and back onto our own. Our 'flaws'. Our imaginary failings.

Odd, too, that the big brands rarely seem to spend as much on researching what their customers might actually want (dresses with backs; tops with fronts; everything with pockets) or how we feel in their stores. Funny how, with all that cash to splash on billboards and supermodel collabs, they don't save a little of it to buy more fabric, so they can stop pretending a size 12 is a legitimate XL. Weird, isn't it, that the clothes we're urged to buy, buy, buy often appear, on closer inspection, not to have been designed for us at all, but some other person with detachable breasts, concave hips and no capacity for intimate chafing? But it can't be the clothes that are wrong, we reason. It must be us.

And it seems pretty likely that the misogyny of fashion, this complicated, antagonistic, love/hate relationship with the clothes on our backs and the shops that flog them, is one of the driving forces behind our over-consumption. It's no coincidence that there is at least seven times more womenswear than menswear in the world's supply of used clothing.[81] Seven times more pressure for us to look 'the part', be sexy or demure, edgy or prim, perfectly put-together or just as precisely undone. Seven times more chance of getting it wrong, and dragging ourselves back to the shops to try again.

If in doubt, let's employ Caitlin Moran's acid test for spotting sexism: ask, 'Are the men doing it?'[82] Are the men participating in fashion? Absolutely, lots of them! But are the men weeping on their bedroom floor because every outfit they put on makes them feel hideous in some new, inarticulable way? Not as far as I've heard. Men might not make us shop, but The Man definitely does.

Of course, the irony is that the time-saving perks of modern shopping are in many ways feminist progression. Just as the arrival of supermarkets marked an end to daily trips round the butcher, baker and grocer with a basket on our arms – now we could buy frozen food once a week and get a job! – so affordable, ready-to-wear clothes released us from a life of darning and drudgery. Everyone who says we should all just go back to the 1930s and sew our own clothes again is forgetting that convenience shopping liberates women, up to a point. But most of us crossed that point a long time ago. Some of us weren't even born.

These days, fashion can feel like an order (buy this!) one minute, and a trick question (Ha! You didn't seriously buy that?') the next. It's the popular girl who invites you to her birthday party, only to lock you in a cupboard and laugh. It's an exam we're constantly failing, that we never chose to sit in the first place.

Still, while women might play a bigger part in fuelling fast fashion, we're also more likely to fight back. The 2018 Ethical Consumer Markets Report found that women were 'much more likely to conduct ethical activities than men', outperforming them in every single purchasing category.[83]

Nobody who has ever used the phrase 'emotional labour', or, y'know, lived in the world with their eyes open, can be surprised by the idea of women worrying more, feeling guiltier or working harder to change their habits. Self-optimisation, they tell us, is the MO of modern womanhood. If we're not trying to shop better then we should be pursuing a better haircut, better health, better friendships, better sleep, better cuticles, or whatever else society has decreed we're failing at this week. To live as a woman often feels like being an outdated operating system, forever resisting the pop-up demands to upgrade ourselves to a whizzier version. There are only so many times we can click 'try again tomorrow' before the pressure gets under our skin.

But I want to believe this could also be a positive thing; women leading the way to a kinder, calmer way of dressing. Because as soon as you start to notice how much money and time and expertise goes into making you want to shop, something magical happens. It undermines that multimillion-pound effort and takes away that illusory power, like seeing the strings above the puppet, or the tiny, wimpy wizard behind the curtain. It's so much more difficult to make someone feel like shit about themselves if they can see how hard you're having to try.

I don't want to quit loving clothes altogether, and I'm guessing you don't either. For all its faults, fashion is a creative force with roots that run through culture, society and identity, far deeper than the fabric on our backs. After all, as more than one person has pointed out to me, lots of us have complex, tricky relationships with food but few of us would choose to eat grey mush at every meal as a better alternative. Buried under all the pressure, there's still pleasure. And it's the pleasure we should be trying to reclaim.

Orsola de Castro, co-founder of Fashion Revolution, sums it up perfectly. 'I love everything about clothes. I love the poetry, I love the fabric, I love the colours, I love the textures,

I love the way that they make you feel. You know, they are our chosen skin.'[84]

'Clothes have such a beautiful power for connecting people,' says Sophie Slater. 'Women have always used clothes to articulate things that they're perhaps not confident articulating. Different cultures, different faiths. I do love dressing up and embodying different characters.'

So do I. Ever since the dressing-up box, clothes have been my chosen creative outlet – but it's the *choosing* that's the most empowering part. And fast fashion, for all its millions of options, can sometimes make us feel like we have no choice at all.

PART TWO: THE SPLIT

Achieving wardrobe closure

THANK U, NEXT

So we need to break up. For the planet, for humankind, for our own sanity, happiness and overdraft. And seeing as the high street isn't likely to instigate the split anytime soon, the most immediate change needs to come from us. We're going to need to do the dumping.

But it's so much easier said than done. For every good intention, there's a 'yes, but . . . '. For every solution, there's a catch. Between balancing environmental impact and human rights, spending more but buying less but still keeping garment workers in (fairly paid) jobs, the whole business of ethical shopping can start to feel a bit like that puzzle where you have to get a wolf, a chicken and a bag of corn across a river.

Take a deep breath. We can only do the best we can do. *But we can probably do better than we are.*

At first, you might find it easiest to go cold turkey. Ghost the high street. Stop answering its calls. Give yourself a finite bracket of time – a month, three months, a year – so there's a finish line to run towards, even if it's a finish line you quietly hope you'll fly over and keep on going.

Never a big one for the 'let's stay friends' charade, this was my route of choice and it was brutal but, ultimately, pretty effective. About halfway through #notnewyear, fast fashion began to feel less of a forbidden fruit, more something I once enjoyed but simply didn't do any more. Like clubbing.

But don't just take my word for it – think about your own personality. Are you a cold turkey kind of person? Do you need absolute, all-or-nothing change to avoid the inevitable backslide? Do you find it a million times easier to say, 'No thanks, I'm not drinking' than 'Okay, but I'm only going to have one'?

Or, are you the type of person who ends up rebelling against your own resolutions like a wayward teen? Would you fare better if you ringfenced one shop or site that you could still use, or created official loopholes? For example: 'I can only buy fast fashion when Mercury is in retrograde', or 'I can go to Zara ONLY on the way back from a smear test'. If you need flexibility, give yourself flexibility. There's no point being a martyr if you're only going to feel deprived and abandon the whole plan within two months flat.

As with any long-term breakup, I'm afraid there is going to be admin. Unsubscribe from all the brands in your inbox. Unfollow every account. And if you want to go one better, tell the brands why you're unfollowing and unsubscribing. I've started typing 'I have stopped buying unsustainable fashion' sniffily into the 'other reason' comment box, in the hope that it might prompt said brand to have an ethical epiphany, sort out their supply chains and give me a £500 gift card as a thank you. I mean, maybe.

But like the clingiest ex, even when you try to cut them out, clothes have a funny way of finding you. Especially these days, when a pair of trousers you clicked on three months ago can stalk you round the internet like some kind of

Wallace and Gromit robot nightmare, hoping to nag you into reconciliation.

Sophie Slater has advice for persistent style crushes. 'If you're addicted to something like Pinterest or Instagram and you see things that you like, make a mental note or write it down,' she says. 'Then go back to your own wardrobe and think, "Have I got something like this already? Do I need it? Is it going to make me happier? What can I style it with? Can I wear it with five other things that are in my wardrobe?"'

These kinds of mental exercises are the bedrock of any fast-fashion breakup, and every sustainability spokesperson out there has their own set of tips and rules to guide you out of the fog and into the light. There are plenty of them over the pages to come, but just to be clear, I'm not going to tell you to buy a bullet journal. At no point will you be required to keep a symptom diary, or make a dream board. Unless that feels like a good way to keep your hands busy.

I am going to tell you to take a long, hard look at yourself, both metaphorically and literally. You're going to need to spend some time looking in a mirror, but you're also going to spend time looking into your . . . *mind mirror*. Or in other words: pay attention to yourself. Notice your own thought patterns. Try to figure out how clothes make you feel, and why you shop the way you do.

The same goes for triggers. You might realise that you always buy regrettable blouses on precisely day three of your period. You could notice the strange urge to go to Monki any time you've had lunch with your mother. You'll begin to talk to your own brain the way you might a grizzly toddler. 'Do you *really* want to try on those velvet dungarees,' you ask, 'or are you just hungry for a snack?'

If you tend to use shopping as a 'treat', try to think up a few alternatives in advance. One of my toughest #notnewyear moments was emerging from the dentist after a hardcore two-hour drilling. As a reward, I would normally shop. A clearance frock, a £6 pair of earrings, some little trinket that would serve more purpose as a consumerist pick-me-up than it ever would in my wardrobe.

'What,' I puzzled, rubbing my numb, drooling face, 'can I do instead?'

The world can be divided neatly into those who will answer this: 'have a nice bath!' and those who will answer: 'masturbate'.

But speaking of self-love, don't be too hard on yourself if you fall off the wagon, because you probably will at some point. Just get back on. A secret midnight ASOS sesh is not the end of the world. But another decade of shopping the way we're shopping? That actually could be.

Holly Bullock is a fashion writer and host of the sustainability-focused podcast *Clothes & The Rest*, and she sees you. 'I think sometimes, when people do a "no-buy challenge", they're sneakily looking for things they can buy when their allotted period of abstinence has ended,' she says.

'In my opinion, it's really important not only to stop making the purchases, but also to stop *thinking* about shopping. It's so liberating to let go of the constant hunt for new things.'

It *is* liberating, and that's the best way to approach all this. Ultimately, you're not depriving yourself by breaking up with fast fashion – you're gaining more freedom. Not to mention money, spare time, self-esteem and cupboard space.

Blogger Ellen Robinson, AKA @ellensinwonderland, likens her sustainable shopping journey to the benchmark altruism study of our times: 'that episode of *Friends* where Phoebe is trying to find a selfless good deed'. Just like donating the $200 that gets Joey on the telethon, quitting fast fashion might feel like pure self-sacrifice at first – but you soon start to reap surprise rewards. 'I feel as though changing my shopping habits has ultimately made me feel better about myself,' she says. 'Making good choices and understanding that you are making a difference has had such a positive impact on my self-confidence.'

And that's good! It's great! Not only is it pretty much impossible to separate the selfish benefits from the selfless, but it's a waste of time to even try. Because one doesn't negate the other. *We are allowed to have both*. We are allowed to make changes for the greater good, and benefit from them personally too.

Some people will change their shopping habits for the planet, some for the people, some for the animals, some because they want to be able to save for a house deposit and some because they want to spend less time feeling shit about their thighs. For most of us it will be a combination of all of those things, and that's fine. Progress is a great multi-tasker. With a swipe of lipstick and a change of shoes, it can take us from work to dinner to dancing.

'It's amazing how blind we can be to the beauty of our own things. Sometimes, it takes a fresh pair of eyes to pick out what's special.'

– Holly Bullock[85]

SORRY BUT YOU'RE GOING TO HAVE TO HAVE A CLEAR-OUT

Believe me, nobody is less happy than I am about me nagging you to tidy your room. Do you think I don't have better things to be doing? For example, tidying my own? But it has to be done, so let's make this as painless as possible. I'm sorry, but you're going to have to have a clear-out.

This is not a radical idea. We are, after all, living in the Age of the Great Declutter. The Streamlining Revolution. The Big Life Edit. From our phone screen to our friends to our spice collection, nowadays we're supposed to prune our lives like an unruly rhododendron, chopping off any part that refuses to bloom. And even as we spend our days accruing more and more stuff, we're already plotting how to get rid of it.

But the idea of a wardrobe cull might sound counterintuitive when you're also trying to give up shopping – like hairdressers insisting that the way to make your hair grow faster is to cut more off. Bear with me. I promise there's logic here.

Firstly, having fewer clothes is one of the most effective ways to ease your decision fatigue. Psychologists and thought leaders have long argued that constraints can make us more creative, and lots of people, the committed 'uniform dressers', find that is true of their wardrobes. Think of it like a Ready Steady Cook bag of clothes. When we're forced to limit ourselves to the same outfits, we get more imaginative – and that creativity is satisfying, which in turn helps dampen the urge to keep shopping.

'Once you can really see what you own, it's much easier to buy less,' says Jade Doherty, @notbuyingnew. 'Since having a capsule wardrobe I've never felt like I've got nothing to wear, which was a frequent feeling before.'

The internet is full of wardrobe detox diets to help you achieve this kind of nouveau-minimalist nirvana – such as Courtney Carver's massively popular Project 333, which challenges you to limit your wardrobe to 33 items or fewer for three months (it sounds like a lot until you discover that accessories, jewellery, coats and shoes all count towards the total). After three months are up, Carver encourages you to reassess your selection and start again, paying attention to the clothes you got the most wear and enjoyment from last time. We learn as we go.

Two months before I stopped shopping, my boyfriend and I moved out of the flat we'd lived in for five years, and into one we'll live in for hopefully even longer. As is the custom, we did a lot of muttered bickering, ate a lot of takeaways and got rid of a lot of extraneous crap. A *lot*. Bag after bag of clothes went to the charity shop or the recycling bin, or, in a few cases, back to its rightful owner.

The culls were not fun, but they were learning exercises. Because in plumbing the murky depths of my wardrobe, I was forced to confront my own habits. When you look at what you haven't worn and think about why that might be, you start to form a clearer picture of your own sartorial successes and failures, the reasons you shop and the emotions that govern your outfit decisions. Then you can spin them into a kind of blueprint for more sensible purchases in the future.

Personally I think this is a much more realistic way to do a wardrobe cull than giving you any set list of rules or criteria, because our clothes are so personal and our reasons for loving, wearing and buying are so subjective. Don't listen to me, listen to *you*. Nobody gives better advice than your past self. And I say that as someone who once queued for an hour with diarrhoea to get into a Shrimps sample sale where the only thing I could afford was a scarf.

For me, vintage pieces have almost always been keepers, partly because they score big with my sentimental side and partly because, by not being on-trend in the first place, they're not as likely to fall off it. Contrary to what people will tell you about plain basics standing the test of time, I've found that really beautiful prints have earned a place. But anything too ubiquitously kitsch – pineapples, flamingoes, palm leaves, storks – has been relegated to the recycling bag. Bold, rich jewel colours have generally stayed in my wardrobe, while neons, pastels and anything in shades Bridget Jones' mother might describe as 'fudges and slurries' have been nixed. Ditto anything sheer, anything box-shaped or anything that requires a weird specialist bra.

Overwhelmingly, all the hasty, zeitgeisty Zara and H&M bits have ended up on the reject pile. Sometimes because they've faded or unravelled; often because they were so precisely evocative of a certain moment in time (ah, the great pom-pom epidemic of '16) that I just couldn't envisage wearing them ever again. If the volume of Zara and H&M in the average charity shop is anything to go by, it's a common theme.

Culling my wardrobe helped me realise that there isn't always a correlation between price and longevity. While I've hung on to expensive things bought because I really loved them, expensive things bought out of any other emotion – boredom, inferiority, because the lady in the boutique said I had nice hair – have generally ended up as guilty cast-offs. Being forced to acknowledge all this is annoying, humbling, but ultimately helpful. You might be pissed off with Past You temporarily for bringing it up, but in the long run you'll be grateful they did.

Anyway, that's the why. Here's the how.

Get all of your clothes out, all of them, and pile them on your bed. Now, step back and marvel at how much there is. Really take it in. Allow yourself to boggle.

Think: 'If I were an alien landing on earth for the first time and I saw this mound of clothes, how many people might I think it belonged to? Five? Ten? A whole village?' Then consider that actually this is very narrow-minded of you, because who are *we* to know whether fast fashion is a problem in other galaxies too? Do we think we're the only intelligent life in the universe capable of shopping ourselves into a planetary crisis? The arrogance! No wonder we're in this mess!

When you are done taking in the sheer volume of clothes you own, in all its almighty grossness, take a deep breath and change tack. Switch to gratitude. Aren't you LUCKY, to have all this? Aren't you fortunate? You, a very ordinary person! You own enough clothes to dress an entire alien village, and all you can do is bitch about needing more of them. Wasn't there a time in your younger life when you'd have killed for a grown-up wardrobe like this; saved up all your pocket money or paper-round money to buy even a piece of it, pored over it in *Sugar* magazine or performed rituals of unspeakable indignity to be allowed to borrow a bit of it off the richest girl at school?

And not just decades ago – how about months ago? Didn't you skip a little bit with happiness as you left the shop holding that top, the one you wore twice and then abandoned because you saw someone wearing it on Loose Women? Those shoes – weren't they your celebration shoes, the ones you bought in a fit of elation the day that really great thing happened?

You told yourself you would always cherish them, didn't you, the Good Day shoes? Then you got a blister and scuffed the suede up a bit and left them under the Christmas decorations box, and to be honest you'd kind of forgotten they even existed. Didn't they deserve a better life, those shoes? Didn't they expect to see a few more Good Days?

You get the idea. You can do this for as long as you have the emotional energy. Try playing music to unlock a special bonus level of introspection. I recommend Joni Mitchell, or Jessie's song from *Toy Story 2*.

But don't let this lovely festival of self-awareness tip over into wallowing. You can't help the clothes by weeping over them, but you can give them a whole new life in the circular economy. You can send them off for someone else to love.

If you want to Kondo, then Kondo to your heart's content. But that's a different book. Personally I'd recommend sorting your clothes into at least four piles:

1) Keep, 2) keep but tweak (i.e. mending and alterations), 3) donate to the charity shop and 4) donate to a textile recycling scheme (although charity shops will often take this pile too).

But you might want to add more categories. Things to sell; things to swap; things to foist off on your friends or family; things to return because they still have the tags on; things to give the dog; things to give the local primary school for its time-capsule project; things to rip up into cleaning cloths. You can divide it up however makes sense to you, but the most important thing is to be honest and ruthless about what you will actually wear.

Interrogate your clothes like they're a bluffing politician and you are Jeremy Paxman. Does it feel good on? Does it itch, or dig in? Does it only look good while standing still, and turn into a strange approximation of an adult nappy the moment you start to walk? Does it have negative emotional associations that you're hoping one day to overcome in a ritual sage-burning ceremony? Were you wearing it when you got dumped by an ex, and are only keeping it so you can give it to Emma Stone's costume designer when she plays you in the movie?

Look at the label. There's no point banishing 'bad' fabrics like polyester once they're already in your wardrobe (the 'already dead' argument for leather is yours if you want it), but you might start to draw some useful conclusions based on certain fibres. Are the dresses you never wear because they make you feel like a moist chipolata all made from PVC-derived synthetics, per chance? Has every foray into linen ended prematurely because of your moral aversion to ironing? Take note.

Don't be tempted to punish yourself by forcing yourself to wear things you don't like, or feel terrible in. That's not what this is about. You need to feel happy and positive about all the clothes you have if you're going to beat the urge to buy more.

And please, don't keep things that don't fit you. Unless they have strong sentimental value or there is a solid reason you'll fit into them in the future, such as giving birth or having a major organ removed, get rid.

But also, be wary of keeping things that *only just* fit. You know, the ones you can zip up at the start of the day that dig in mercilessly by lunchtime. I have far too many of these things. Morning trousers. Post-menstrual skirts. Either you wear them and feel miserable all day, or you don't wear them and you feel guilty about it. Life is too short, so bag those up too. An outfit should always have at least 20 per cent space for pasta.

I'm pretty sure Diana Vreeland said that.

'The most sustainable garment is the one already in your wardrobe.'

– Orsola de Castro[86]

THIRTY, FLIRTY AND THRIVING

The #30Wears challenge was started by ethical campaigner Livia Firth, co-founder of consultancy Eco Age, as a rule of thumb for more sustainable shopping. Before you buy anything, ask yourself: will I wear it thirty times?

It's a very good deterrent to stop you buying clothes you can't commit to (think you'll wear white leather culottes once a week for the next seven months, do ya?), but it's also helpful as a retroactive way to examine your shopping errors. Look at the clothes you own that you have worn thirty times, and ask yourself why. Is it a certain fabric or colour you always go back to? A certain shape or historical reference you love? Have more expensive, classic pieces fared better in the cutthroat world of your wardrobe, or are kooky vintage items the ones you never seem to get bored of?

Which isn't to say you need to fill your whole wardrobe solely with that colour or fabric or label or those kooky vintage items, but it'll start to give you a better idea of the purpose clothes serve, *really* serve, in your life.

When you've done that, flip it. Go through the clothes you're getting rid of, and ask 'why?' with all the persistence of a needy preschooler. Why didn't you wear it thirty times? Why didn't you wear it ten, or even five times? The days you put it on and took it off again, would *they* add up to thirty? Or did you barely even take it off the hanger?

Beware the excuses. 'I'd have worn it thirty times if the weather were better'; 'I'd have worn it thirty times if I got invited to more parties'; 'I'd have worn it thirty times if Amanda had had another twenty-nine hen weekends.'

But don't dwell; learn from the low-scorers, and aim higher next time. Hold that magic number in your head as you shop, and force yourself do the maths before you reach for your wallet. If you're going to wear a top thirty times, that means you need to wear it roughly once every twelve days for a year, or just over once a month for two years. Can you imagine that? Would you still be happy in the top by wear #29, or would your affection start to wane around wear #7? What if this rule were somehow enforceable by law?

The result is probably going to mean buying far fewer things, and walking away from many more. But the ones you do buy will be so much better. If there's one thing everyone, *everyone*, says, it's that your thirties are great. I choose to believe them.

*'Surrealism is the magical surprise of finding a lion in a
wardrobe, where you were "sure" of finding shirts.'*

– Frida Kahlo[87]

SOMETIMES IT'S OKAY TO LEAVE THEM HANGING

I am about to be quite controversial . . . hold on to your
hats!

No, that's it – hold on to your hats. And scarves, jackets,
jumpers, shoes. The received wisdom when it comes to sustainable shopping is usually to cull your clothes based on
when you last wore them, until you have whittled it down to
the perfect capsule wardrobe. But I'm here to be the madcap renegade who says . . . *not necessarily.*

There's no doubt nixing half your wardrobe can be good for
the soul, as well as plenty of other things beginning with
dust allergies and ending with your relationship. Science is
onside too: neuroscientists have found that physical clutter
competes for our attention, making us less productive, more
easily distracted and more irritable[88]. It can negatively
impact levels of life satisfaction, especially as we get older.[89]

But that's clutter. Clutter denotes things with no place or
practical purpose. If your clothes become clutter then

perhaps you don't need them – or perhaps you need to reinstate them as not-clutter instead. Find them a place, give them an iron and rediscover what their practical purpose might be.

We hang on to clothes we don't wear for all kinds of reasons, both practical and emotional. Not least because fashion is (all together now!) a bastard. People often tell you to get rid of any clothes you haven't worn in the last year, but that always strikes me as a rash approach when trends are so cyclical and inclined to about-turn. A year is not a long time. There's a strong argument to be made for keeping some things on the bench for many years, because their time will come again. Let's call them your garmy reserves.

More than once I've sent an item to the charity shop, only to regret it later when the right outfit or occasion finally came along. That embroidered vintage shirt I told you about, with the voluminous sleeves? When I bought it, I had a sudden hankering to wear it beneath a short-sleeved fitted jumper and a beret. It would be adorable! Witty! French! I became obsessed with the idea. But I didn't have a short-sleeved fitted jumper. I used to – a lovely and only slightly holey cashmere one that had sat at the bottom of a drawer for years – but I'd got rid of it during my most recent wardrobe cull. I had to hunt down a similar one on eBay. That was annoying.

Many other times I've dug something ancient out of the wardrobe, thinking, 'Oh, actually!' Now I've got the right skirt to go with it, or the right shoes, or the right friends, or the Lazy Susan of trends has nudged it back round the table. Any time we buy anything new, the existing clothes in our wardrobe transmogrify, just slightly, in relation to it. The top you were bored of four years ago might suddenly look good again. The shoes that went with nothing might finally have purpose. It's always worth taking time to try your newer stuff on with your old, old dregs.

Some of us are natural collectors and some of us aren't, but also some things earn their right to be kept, and others don't. The challenge is working out which is which.

So ask yourself: if I slipped into a coma right now and woke up at a time when this style or shape or colour was all the rage again, wouldn't I want to go out and buy a better version? Is THIS the one I would be happy to wear? If the answer is no, it can go. Although not without a moment of musing on why you bought something you didn't really like in the first place.

But if the answer is yes, and you have the space, keep it. At least for a while longer. If you hold it and feel warm, fond feelings towards it, if perhaps a little montage of you and the item skipping through a meadow or having a picnic or stumbling home from a great party or whatever pops into your mind, then don't get rid. Fashion changes. Life does too. And just like a weak pun on the phrase 'hold onto your hats' that I jotted down years ago, you never know when it might come in useful.

RAIL AGAINST THE SYSTEM

Something else I've found incredibly helpful, although it started off as an unintentional stopgap because I moved flat and didn't own any furniture, is using freestanding clothes rails instead of a wardrobe.

Now, this might offend your design sensibilities, or not work for numerous practical reasons – but if it's an option you're considering then I really recommend it. As well as sparing us IKEA flatpack hell, the rails come with all kinds of benefits.

For one thing, there's only a finite amount of space. When they're full, they're full, and liable to collapse on my head in the night, so it's an extra incentive to keep a lid on the #not-new shopping.

For another thing, having the bulk of my wardrobe out in the open rather than stashed away in a cupboard means that in the morning, when I'm doing the frantic 'WHY DON'T I HAVE ANY CLOTHES?' bit, I'm immediately confronted by the truth. I DO have clothes. And look, there they are! I can see the whole spectrum of options I possess every day, in all its glorious, technicolour variety. And while not every day is going to be a leopard devorée day or a monochrome capelet day, it's still cheering, as I'm pulling on the same jumper and jeans for the third day running, to remember that they're there.

Remembering things are there is often half the problem, isn't it? Clothes rails don't allow you the luxury of forgetting what you own, and there's nowhere to hide an unreturned haul. The very innards of my wardrobe are exposed, and with them my mistakes and triumphs. Neglected clothes eyeball me in the morning, prompting me to bust out of my outfit ruts – and even if I don't reach for them, they're still fulfilling a more decorative purpose than they would be inside a wardrobe. Can I call them art? Let's call them art. Great clothes deserve to be seen.

Great clothes also deserve to be cared for, and the rails force me to do that better too. I'm obliged to hang things up properly every evening, on the space-saving velvet hangers I also recommend (they're grippy). I can't slam a door shut and pretend I didn't see things fall on the floor.

Obviously if you want to stick to a wardrobe for aesthetic, practical or lion-and-witch-related reasons, that's fair enough. I'm not being sponsored by a clothes rail manufacturer, I promise (like all the best things in life, mine was free off Facebook Marketplace).

But I do feel obliged to tell you, if you're keeping your clothes behind closed doors, to keep them tidy. Colour-code them, file them from formal to casual, or organise them in some other way that makes most sense for your brain and life – but at least try to make them orderly and accessible enough that you can open your wardrobe doors, step back in the middle of your 'WHY DON'T I HAVE ANY CLOTHES?' moments, and realise that you DO have clothes. Loads of them. Look! There they are.

A season, a reason, a lifetime

When there are fifty-two seasons on the high street and god-knows-what happening in the weather forecast, I'm aware this might sound archaic. But if you've got space in the loft or under the bed, might I suggest separating out your height-of-summer/depths-of-winter clothes?

If nothing else, it makes sense not to keep everything you own in one jumbled mass when you won't wear some of it for eight months a year. Packing all the bulky jumpers or the holiday kaftans away could also help in your bid to better appreciate what you have. I can see clearly now the coats are gone, etc.

But also, I love the big seasonal wardrobe switcheroo. Along with Pancake Day, Eurovision and New Purse/Old Purse Changeover Day, it is one of the most underrated calendar occasions.

I love the ceremony and ritual of it, going through my old steamer trunk and welcoming the coats and jumpers back into rotation. 'How've you been, old pals? Great to see you Fuzzy Bob, looking cosy as ever. How was storage this summer, did you get much good air? Parka Pete, welcome back! Brenda! I forgot I even had you! C'mere Snuggles, I've missed you the most.'

A little more ceremony and ritual can be helpful when it comes to loving our clothes for longer, I think. Rediscovering old favourites is a good way to quell that 'new season, must shop!' panic that always kicks in around the first chime of the ice cream van or the first whiff of pumpkin spice. When you haven't seen something in six months, it can feel almost new.

It's also a good prompt for a wardrobe audit. If a flamingo-print romper complete with Maxibon stains doesn't make you vow to shop more wisely this summer, nothing will.

'Care for your clothes, like the good friends they are.'

– Joan Crawford, *My Way Of Life*[91]

SUDS' LAW

Not much of this process will be easy, but here's one part that is: stop washing your clothes as often.

Most of us are too clean anyway. You've probably heard theories about modern germaphobia being the cause of childhood allergies ('In my day we fed them a dirt sandwich every morning and sent them off to play in a dung heap!'), while the rise in 'intimate hygiene' products has been widely damned as yet another attempt by capitalism to cash in on female insecurity. Humans are living, breathing, walking ecosystems, covered in microbes and gook. We don't need to be sterilised like a kitchen counter, and nor do our clothes.

Not least because up to 25 per cent of each garment's carbon footprint comes from the way we wash and care for it.[92] Every time we wash plastic-based fabrics like polyester and nylon, they shed thousands of tiny fibres which then contaminate our waterways, rivers and oceans and end up ingested by fish – and by us. Microplastic particles have been found in 83 per cent of drinking water from twelve countries around the world, including the UK, and the risks to human health are still a big unknown.[93]

We do know that washing and drying a load of laundry every two days creates a carbon footprint of around 440kg of CO_2e each year, which is 'equivalent to flying from London to Glasgow and back with 15-mile taxi rides to and from the airports' – and nearly three quarters of that comes from the tumble dryer.[94] If you have outdoor space, six months of hanging clothes on the line to dry instead could save 700lbs of greenhouse gases.[95] Plus no pants stuck to the inside of your trouser leg. In 2017, WRAP announced that our carbon footprint had been reduced by 700,000 tonnes of CO_2e in five years through people washing their clothes at lower temperatures (there's rarely a reason you should need to go above 30°), and ironing and tumble drying less frequently.[96] This stuff really does make a difference.

And pollution isn't the only reason to start employing the sniff test. Washing our clothes less frequently is a proven way to prolong their lifespan. Think of all the jumpers you've lost to shrinkage, the prints that faded, the fabrics that were never quite the same after that first spin. All those wardrobe heroes, taken too soon. It might be evidence that fashion quality is declining, but it's also a terrible waste of good outfits.

What needs or doesn't need washing is always going to be a subjective matter – one person's gravy stain is another's 'decorative motif' – and barring lost luggage or a surprise sleepover situation, let's agree that underwear, socks and anything else worn *intimately* should still be washed after every wear. But for everything else, stop and evaluate. Does it really need full immersion, or is this something a little squirt of stain remover could fix? An hour or two airing on the washing line? An evening on a radiator, or hanging in a steamy bathroom?

There's even Day2 Dry Wash Spray, which is pretty much dry shampoo for clothes and every bit as life-changing as that sounds. It neutralises odours, smoothes creases and softens fabric without washing. Each bottle, the company claims, has the potential to save around 60 litres of water, but it also has the potential to save your favourite dress from becoming a bobbly, misshapen shadow of its former self. They make a version designed for delicates too, which is a godsend for what I call 'summer bra syndrome': those weeks in July and August where your laundry schedule is dictated by your underboob sweat.

But if all this is going to work then we need to wash out a few societal norms as we go. Can we make a hint of rumpled grubbiness cool again, like it was in the 60s? Or at the very least, remember we are all animals too? We're just big sacks of organic matter, perpetually shedding and renewing and brewing. We're not supposed to look boxfresh at all times.

As a person who only very recently learned that you're supposed to clean washing machines (but they're self-cleaning! Like vaginas!), I admit I may not be best qualified – but please, let me be the first – to say: you can get another day out of that. I promise, I can't smell a thing.

'I need to live in a land where people can spill.'

– Phoebe Buffay[97]

OUT, DAMNED SPOT

I'd estimate that at any given moment, around 40 per cent of my clothes have food on them.

If you're nodding because you assume I have young children, I do not. I have a big appetite, no patience and a chronic inability to keep napkins on my lap. But while spillage is an inevitable part of a life well lived (they're just friendly food ghosts! Lunch souvenirs!), stains are also one of the sloppiest and saddest reasons we let our clothes fall out of circulation. Here lies a once-loved top. Cause of death: extra guacamole.

But it's a preventable death, if you act fast enough. Here are five DIY stain saviours to try when you're caught on the hop.

(Number six is a bib.)

1. Oil

Quick, fetch talcum powder. Or, if an elderly aunt hasn't been to stay recently, try corn flour or dry shampoo. Apply a generous amount of powder to the stain and leave it for a few hours to fully absorb the oil. Scrape it off, give the stain a gentle scrub with cold water and soap or washing-up liquid. Repeat if needed. Finish your spaghetti.

2. Red wine

Anecdotal evidence suggests the white wine thing *does* work, but don't waste good Grigio until you've tried this first. Blot the stain gently (don't rub it in further), then apply a heap of salt and leave it to absorb the wine. You can also use bicarbonate of soda to the same effect, but they're less likely to have that in the pub.

3. Berries

Turn inside out, pull the fabric taut and pour boiling water (or the hottest water you can access) through the stain from behind. Yes, take it off first. For stains on cotton, you can also try rubbing in a little whitening toothpaste with a toothbrush, then rinsing.

4. Chocolate

Turn the fabric over and hold it under the cold tap to loosen the stain particles from the back. If you can't take the item off, saturate the stain as best you can with cold water (it's best to avoid heat with any fat or protein-based stains, as it will cause them to bake even further into the fabric), then massage in a little detergent, soap or washing-up liquid. Work your way from the outside of the stain inwards, and repeat if needed until the stain is gone.

5. Blood

Follow the same steps as above – flush the stain out with cold water from the back of the fabric, or immerse in cold water as fully as possible. Then apply detergent or soap and rub, rub, rub. For dried-in blood stains you might need to try something stronger; white vinegar should do the trick (soak for thirty minutes and rinse in cold water), or dab with hydrogen peroxide. But be very careful using it on anything delicate, like silk or lace. Occasionally, 'dry-clean only' labels aren't lying.

'In the rush to own things for reasons of status and looks,
we lose the opportunity to be mindful and resourceful
through the act of making and creating.'

– Jane Milburn[98]

STITCHIN' IS BITCHIN'
(and other reasons to thread a needle)

One of the most treasured things in my wardrobe is a homemade top. The fabric, smooth cotton in a retro yellow-and-brown leaf print, was bought by my late Auntie Elsie from Whiteleys of Bayswater in 1964. I know this because I have the receipt. Both were passed on to me when I was fifteen, in the middle of my DT Textiles GCSE, with the suggestion that I might help the fabric fulfil its long-awaited destiny to become clothes.

Because I'm lazy and impatient, I turned Auntie Elsie's fabric into the easiest thing I could think of – a top, made in a square like a cushion cover, tied up at the bottom with a sash and at the top with a halterneck. It didn't have a zip, because I couldn't do zips, so I would wiggle in and out of it via the time-honoured method of almost dislocating my shoulder. It was crude, and the seams were wonky, but it made the beautiful fabric wearable and that felt like the most important thing. Auntie Elsie lived to 102 and the top seems to have inherited her longevity, that leaf print just as lovely now as it was in '64 and '03.

My sewing skills, meanwhile, have slipped. A lot. I no longer have a machine, just an old box filled with thread in weird colours and two decades' worth of spare buttons in little plastic packets. My efforts are held together with determination, imagination and, very occasionally, superglue. But even so, as I've moved away from fast fashion, I've found myself more and more reliant on my shit sewing kit. It's got me out of many tight spots, and I mean that quite literally.

Beyond my sofa craft sessions, a renaissance is afoot. More than a million people (nearly all women) took up sewing between 2014 and 2017,[99] with Hobbycraft reporting a 60 per cent rise in sales of sewing and knitting patterns in 2016.[100] The BBC's *The Great British Sewing Bee* has audiences hooked, offering the same soothing recipe of incredible talent, homespun humility and unlikely intergenerational friendship as *Bake Off* before it.

But it's not just nostalgia for petticoat fetishists. Dressmaking is shaping up as a thoroughly modern hobby. There has been a shift towards 'mindful' sewing, knitting and handicrafts as one of the many ways millennials are attempting to log out, switch off and recharge our tech-frazzled brains. A distinct advantage of sewing over, say, adult colouring books or taking a lot of long baths is that you have something useful to show for your efforts at the end of it.

And, of course, if fast fashion is the devil then home sewing is the saintly alternative; the growing-your-own-marrows of the sustainable clothing world. It's pure free-range creativity unsullied by capitalist greed. Or mostly, anyway.

'I had one woman who came to a sewing class and said she wanted to learn to sew so that she could buy clothes off ASOS, copy them and then send them back,' laughs Charlotte Newland, winner of *The Great British Sewing Bee* 2016. 'Actually said it, out loud. We all just stared.' Since her time on the show she's become a TV presenter, sewing teacher and craft ambassador, with a loyal following of enthusiastic home sewists (they prefer this to 'sewers' for obvious reasons).

Most of Newland's students have more honorable motivations than ripping off fast fashion, but they aren't all doing it for the ethical kudos. More often, she tells me, it's because they want to learn to make something that fits them properly, and escape the tyranny of high-street sizing. Jeans are especially popular. 'People say, "Oh my god, they look like 'proper jeans'!" – and of course they do. Anyone can make them, it just takes three days.'

Personally, I'd give up three weeks for a pair of jeans that actually fit.

Still, there's no beating the clock: in the world of 'slow' fashion, sewing it yourself is the slowest option of all. But that patience is all part of the process; an investment of time and energy that represents your commitment to the garment, and means you're more likely to treasure it afterwards. You don't spend three days making something you're only going to wear once. Besides, if we add up all those hours we've spent on fruitless high-street missions, wrestling ourselves in and out of things that fit badly and start to lose their appeal even before we've got the zip up, an evening or two at a sewing machine begins to sound like a spa day by comparison.

Newland has barely set foot on the high street for the past four years, aside from tights or the occasional bra. She even makes her own knickers from fabric offcuts. 'It's wonderful. I don't miss the changing room hell, I don't miss being beholden to trends. I'm too old for that bollocks,' she says. 'I never really got it, to be honest. I couldn't compete. Fashion always felt like a competition that I just couldn't win.'

While some keen sewists use their skills to stay one step ahead of the industry, for many it's liberating to drop out of the race altogether. Sewing your own clothes means not having to wait for your preferred trouser shape or neckline to come back round again, like a suitcase on a luggage carousel. It means you can craft things to celebrate your body and make you feel like the best version of yourself, not . . . well, like a suitcase on a luggage carousel.

'I'm quite an unusual shape. Or rather—' Charlotte catches herself, '98 per cent of us are not the shape *decreed that we should be* by fashion. But I always found it so hard to buy dresses, because I have big boobs, no waist and small hips. I'm like a sausage. Things would never fit right. But now I can make things that fit perfectly.'

It's the same philosophy Mandie Voukanari credits with the success of her business, Lofty Frocks, making made-to-measure custom dresses out of repurposed vintage fabric. 'My clients love the personal service,' she says. 'To find a dress that fits all parts of the body can be challenging, as let's face it, who has a one-size body?'

I first came across @LoftyFrocks on Instagram in 2015, when I ordered a sundress made from candy-striped 80s bedsheets, and explained in great detail over email that I needed a long bodice, as my boobs tend to leave waistbands hovering somewhere around my armpits. She skilfully obliged. The dress fits like a glove, and it cost me £75.

Voukanari tells me that growing awareness around sustainability is increasingly driving business, but it's the bespoke results that really bring the love. 'I cannot tell you the amount of messages I have received thanking me for making them feel good about themselves,' she says. 'It makes me want to cry with happiness.'

But even the cosy world of sewing isn't unfailingly inclusive. Nice plus-size dressmaking patterns can be hard to find (something to do with needing a different 'block', although I can't tell you what that means), which is an especially unfair kicker for women who are making their own clothes *specifically* because the high street makes them feel unwelcome.

Author, plus-size fashion influencer and now-sewist Bethany Rutter has spoken about the irony. 'It's been really interesting, entering this world that's meant to kind of liberate me by giving me more choice of what I can make, and make stuff that doesn't exist, but then finding that the same dynamic exists in the sewing world as the ready-to-wear fashion world,' she told comedian Sofie Hagen last year on the *Made of Human* podcast.[101] 'I'm yet to receive a satisfactory answer on why it isn't just a question of making [patterns] bigger ... I would like pattern designers to be more mindful of who they're catering to, and ask themselves "why not?"'

Another limitation of dressmaking is the price. Fabric isn't cheap, nor are patterns, nor are workshops and courses – and it's no secret that making a dress from scratch can cost more than a high-street equivalent. 'It is expensive,' Newland agrees. But she subscribes to the same philosophy as lots of slow-fashion champions: 'That's how much it *should* cost. We need to adjust that mindset.'

People say you should only eat meat if you'd be prepared to kill the animal yourself. Should we have a similar rule for clothes? You can only buy a £25 dress if you know how hard it is to make one?

Happily there are ways to keep costs down and sustainable kudos up – like Lofty Frocks' vintage fabric library, or the growing numbers of free patterns and tutorials available to download from sites like Hobbycraft and so-sew-easy.com. You can always do a Sound of Music with an old pair of curtains (try charity shops), or follow the lead of blogger Kari Greaves, @east_london_style, who upcycles vintage finds into entirely new pieces, like a kind of glam high-fashion Dr Frankenstein. In her hands, a frou-frou 80s wedding dress becomes a chic party frock. Moth holes become windows of opportunity. An Iron Maiden T-shirt and a lace petticoat become one beautiful hybrid creation. She dyes, she chops, she trims, and when she gets bored, she does it all over again.

'I personally became disillusioned with how fast fashions came and went and it seemed so much effort was put into clothing, especially older pieces, and then disregarded so quickly,' she tells me. Although her transformations are sometimes met with puritanical outrage ('even from friends!'), they're proof that DIY fashion doesn't have to feel like a step back in time. And nor does vintage. 'I believe that being able to reuse something rather than it be left to rot is so much better,' she says. Agreed. Reduce, reuse, recycle – and reap the rewards.

Although we might want to stop just short of my friend's grandmother, who was so fanatical about repurposing old clothes that once, on a picnic, she offered 'something to wipe your hands with' and produced a pair of her husband's old pants from her bag. There are limits.

Craft isn't history, although it can be heritage. Craft is alive.'

– Simone Cipriani, founder of the Ethical Fashion Initiative[102]

ON THE MEND

While we can all agree that the return to dressmaking is a lovely thing, let's be honest – the majority of us are not going to start sewing our own clothes from scratch. We just aren't. It's a skill anyone can learn, albeit with the privilege of time, money and space, but then so is tennis or playing the flute and we probably aren't going to do those either.

But even if we can't picture ourselves ever rustling up a pair of slacks from an old bedspread, there are other reasons to cotton on. I'm not about to urge you to turn your old jeans into a funky tote bag or craft a skirt entirely out of old ties, but I am going to advocate for learning a few amateur sewing skills.

Because the death of mending is a big problem, and not just in fashion. Appliances, furniture, technology, opinions – rather than fix them, we're quick to throw them out and get a new one.

Even if we're in it for the long haul, big business has us over a barrel, making it easier and often cheaper to replace things than repair them, so we have to keep on buying more. You know the way your iPhone goes all slow and pathetic, like clockwork, four months before your contract is up? We might call it a ball-ache; activists call it planned obsolescence. 'It's basically part of the apparatus of capitalism, that when something breaks then we have to replace it constantly,' explains Sophie Slater. 'Clothing is just the next in that line.'

While spending more doesn't always guarantee better quality, most of the people I've spoken to agree that the rise of cheap, fast fashion has corresponded with a decline in longevity. Brands don't have the incentive to produce clothes that last ten years if we're only buying them to wear for ten months, or ten minutes. So they just don't make 'em like they used to. Which means more waste in landfill, more recycling to process, more rubbish to be digested one way or another by a planet that's already too full.

Still, we don't have to lie down and accept our unravelling hems and frayed cuffs as an inevitable prompt to go shopping.

'Find a great tailor!' is advice you'll hear a lot from ethical ambassadors, and they're absolutely right, even if it does sound like saying 'find a great chauffeur!'. Most dry-cleaners will alter clothes for as little as a tenner, and can mend wear and tear with wizard-like precision.

But in case going to a tailor sounds like too much effort, or, frankly, feels a bit too *Fast Show*, there's a groundswell of startups hoping to meet us in the middle, using modern tech to facilitate old-fashioned methods. The Clothes Doctor app lets you arrange repairs, cleaning and alterations via your phone. Simply post your clothes to their Cornwall workshop and get them back within seven to ten days. The Restory will rejuvenate shoes and bags with all the finesse of a Harley Street surgeon. Its non-judgemental treatment list includes stretching out the too-small shoes you bought anyway ('my feet are just swollen from walking around all day!') and cleaning mystery stains off the handbag you should never have put on the floor of that pub toilet. And for every swish atelier featured in *Tatler*, there are at least three more reliable, reasonably-priced sewing businesses wising up and going digital. In five years' time, I'm hopeful we'll all be able to book a trouser-hemming or a trainer-restoration with all the greedy ease of Deliveroo.

For now, though, the simplest and cheapest option is still to do it yourself. While it's hard to fix your own broken TV without proper training, mending our clothes is something most of us could manage with little more than a YouTube tutorial and a hotel sewing kit. We could sew up holes, replace buttons, reinforce unravelling seams and patch up the worn-out crotch of our best-loved jeans. We could do it right now, instead of putting the trashed clothes away in a drawer to rediscover in a rush another morning.

We don't even have to do it neatly. There's a whole 'visible mending' movement, driven by the belief that repairs can elevate a garment to a whole new aesthetic level. The ancient Japanese art of *sashiko* is all the rage among modern-day sewists and quilters, using thick, contrasting thread (traditionally white on dark fabric) to turn repairs into mini works of art, with bold geometric patterns in stitching that's supposed to be seen. Denim patches were big for that brief period in 2017, but perhaps they deserve a more permanent place in our wardrobes. Liz Hurley's Versace safety-pin moment could have a budget revival. Necessity is the mother of invention, and out of constraints come great creativity. Today I noticed a crucial button was missing from my blouse and was forced to improvise with an earring. You see? Fixing things is not beyond us! We can laugh in the face of planned obsolescence.

And if you're prepared to alter your clothes, even just a little bit, it opens up a much wider pool to choose from. Vintage and charity shopping becomes so much more viable knowing you can have things altered to suit your life, mood or the changing winds of fashion. And a few basic DIY tricks can make a huge difference when it comes to extending the useful life of your wardrobe.

'I'll never find time,' you think, but you will. Because now you have the time you used to spend shopping.

Can we fix it?

Yes we can.

A bobbly jumper

Very (*very*) gently shave the bobbles off with a razor. Not the same one you just used on your legs.

A stiff zip

Rub a pencil up and down the metal teeth – the graphite will lubricate them and help it run more smoothly.

An exposed bra underwire

Wrap duct tape or a plaster around the end of the underwire to stop it poking through again, then push it back as far into the bra as you can. Either stitch the hole closed, or stick a section of medical cushioned tape over the hole. The heat from your body will help it adhere.

Scuffed suede

You can buy a specialist suede eraser (Jason Markk makes a good one), or just use a pencil eraser to gently buff out marks.

A shrunken jumper

Soak in lukewarm water and hair conditioner for a few hours, then push out the excess water, lay it on a towel and gently – *gently* – stretch it back to its original size. This should work, unless the wool has become 'felted'. In which case you might have to bid farewell to your jumper, and say hello to some free felt! Remember the golden rule of wardrobe maintenance: a disaster is just a craft project you haven't met yet.

'I base my fashion taste on what doesn't itch.'

– Gilda Radner[103]

CUTTING CORNERS

You can't be too precious about clothes.

That might sound at odds with everything I've said up to now about cherishing and preserving them. And certainly you *can't* be too precious when it comes to forging an emotional attachment, honouring their origins and not wrecking them in the wash. But what I mean is: don't be afraid to make them work for you.

Don't be afraid to make them work for you, *with scissors.*

You bought it, you own it, it's yours for the tweaking. You can't worry about hurting the feelings of some unknown designer. Trust me, nobody is going to leap out of a cupboard and tell you off for making their clothes more wearable. Mr New Look doesn't know where you live.

Many clothes never get worn enough to even make it to the repair stage. The could-wear-don't-wears. The gapers, the saggers and the rider-uppers. The tops that don't work with any bra known to humanity, and the trousers with turn-ups that won't stay turned up. Clothes you put on thinking, 'This! Why don't I wear this more often?' and then remember exactly why, but only after it's too late to go back and change.

All too often we feel that if clothes don't fit perfectly then we somehow don't deserve them. As though our bodies have failed fashion, not the other way round. But a tiny, easy fix can be all it takes to make clothes work for you, rather than against you. The difference between a garment that gets worn and a garment that gets wasted can be as small as snipping off an itchy label, or a pair of hanger loops that are always protruding from the neckline (hanger loops and I have been engaged in a violent grudge match since about 1997). It could be as tiny as stitching a collar so it lies perfectly flat, or moving a button an inch to display exactly your preferred amount of cleavage. Shortening the slightly too-long bag strap that falls off your shoulder as you fumble for your keys every damn day. Buying a slip to go under that staticky skirt, so you can stop hoiking it out from between your legs every three paces.

Personally, my favourite trick is to combat boob-gape in button-down shirts and dresses by simply sewing them up. I'm going to write that again, slowly, so you can process the revelation. Just. Sew. Them. Up. One small stitch on the middle seam; one giant leap for bosomy womankind.

You still need to be able to get in and out, of course, so check wriggle-room as you go and only sew between the necessary buttons – but frankly, a few seconds of amateur escapology in the evening are worth it to be able to go about your day safely contained.

If you can't sew it up, there are press studs. Hooks and eyes. Iron-on velcro. These are all, I promise you, better solutions for gaping buttons than giving up and resorting to that eternal symbol of big-titted defeat: the camisole. In really desperate times (always weddings) I've even sewn my bra *to* my dress to keep everything in check. Delicately extracting myself at 2am post-Proseccos is Future Lauren's problem.

Then there's Wundaweb, also known as Bondaweb, the patron saint of lazy menders everywhere. Wundaweb is a roll of mesh tape adhesive that you iron between two layers of fabric to fuse them together. Use it to fix hems that have come unravelled, turn-ups that won't stay turned up, cuffs that you want rolled back just-so, and wrap dresses that threaten to fly open in the middle of a christening. It works almost instantly, costs approximately 50 times less than a sewing machine and, if you're really a woman after my own heart, you can do it with your hair straighteners.

Once you start seeing the modification potential in your wardrobe, it's hard to stop. The internet is an invaluable trove of video tutorials and step-by-step guides on every tailoring trick you could imagine, with gurus to suit every style and ability level, from hip fashion students to bouffanted midwestern moms. You can become your own personal couturier, making clothes bespoke and perfectly fitted to your body. You can sew a bra into a backless dress, laughing in the face of gravity. You can add splices to make a midi skirt feel less 'vicar's wife'. You can turn long tops and shirts into bodysuits, so they never billow out from your waistband again. It involves cutting the gusset out of an old pair of knickers, but that's a small price to pay for a life free from tucking.

I mean, be careful; don't blunder in drunk and start wrecking half your wardrobe. But do not be afraid. You are the architect of your own destiny, and you're allowed to dictate the length of your own denim shorts. I realise that telling you to make jeans into cut-offs might be stating the blindingly obvious, but then it's amazing how often the obvious escapes us.

One of my favourite jumpers – a #30Wears champion, possibly rounding in on a cool #50Wears – is a forest-green rollneck in sweatshirt material, stolen from my Gran's house when we cleared it out ready to be sold a couple of years ago. It started off a suitably grannyish length, as a tunic that came right down past my bum. Presumably to be worn with a nice pair of crease-front slacks to a rotary meeting, I don't know. I loved the colour, fabric and fit, and I loved that it had been hers. But because I'm not in the habit of wearing tunics, I spent the first year I had it attempting to shove acres of its thick sweatshirt fabric into skirt waistbands and smoothing it into high-waisted jeans, where it would roll up within five minutes and look like a rogue piece of tubing had got caught.

Were it not for the sentimental association, I might have just given up on the jumper. But instead, finally, I had an epiphany and chopped it off. I hemmed it, with a single row of wonky hand stitching, in front of the TV. It took about an hour.

Now it sits exactly on my waist, slightly longer at the back than the front so I get the illusion of the sainted 'French tuck' without all the smoothing and bunching. It looks great with pretty much all my skirts and trousers, and also over dresses. I wear it endlessly.

She's still around, by the way, my granny. I also pilfered a shell-print silk scarf, a handmade beach top and a heavy navy pea coat from her in the big clearout, and I delight in wearing them when I go to visit her in her care home. She delights in it too, I think. There's something special about working those souvenirs of her life into my own, adapting them, translating them and giving them fresh purpose. Especially as they're not valuable heirlooms; they're every-day clothes that could just as easily have ended up in the recycling bag. It goes to prove that at least half of the joy of clothes is in the meaning we give them. We reap back the value we invest.

And Granny doesn't seem to mind that I butchered her jumper. Or if she does then she's being polite.

'Repetition is not repetition. The same action makes you feel something completely different by the end.'

– Pina Bausch[104]

BUT THEY'VE SEEN ME IN IT BEFORE!

In the long mental list of criteria we go through when getting dressed in the morning, this is one of the more illogical doozies.

'I'll wear the orange jumper', you think, having squared the orange jumper with enough other points on the list to make it a viable OOTD. But then, you think again. What were you wearing the last time this person saw you? It was the orange jumper, wasn't it? It was. It was the orange sodding jumper.

And so the orange jumper is automatically vetoed. You can't wear the orange jumper again, because what the hell will they think? That you only have one outfit? That you've been co-opted into a cult, or a prison knitting circle? Become a full-time Velma from Scooby Doo impersonator? You'll have to blurt out the universal explainer – 'I was wearing this last time I saw you! You must think I have no clothes AHAHAHAHA' – in a desperate attempt to own the situation before anyone else owns you.

And if you're seeing a whole group of people, or going to more than one thing with more than one person who has at one time or another seen you wearing clothes, the problem is multiplied. If you happen to be wearing it on the same day of the week as last time ('You must think I always wear orange jumpers on Wednesdays!') or to the exact same place ('You must think this is my Wagamama jumper!') it only gets worse. Suddenly you're engaged in a kind of impossible outfit sudoku, trying to work out which clothes will be the least repetitive to the largest number of people.

We need to stop doing this. Not least because it's seriously hampering our ability to leave the house on time in the morning, but also because it's forever reinforcing the idea that new clothes = good, and old clothes = bad. Every time we do it, the wardrobe sudoku, much as we may resent it, we're complicit.

The good news is that we *can* stop doing this, for two reasons.

1) People do not remember your clothes. They just don't. Unless your friends are the collected staff of *Hello!* magazine and you are Kate Middleton in a coat dress. People. Don't. Remember.

If you don't believe me, think about the number of times a person has said 'I like that! Is it new?' and you've wanted to list the many times they've seen you in it before, aghast that the vision wasn't seared onto their memory like a panini press. Sometimes the person who says this will be a person you are dating, or a person you live with. Sometimes the outfit they don't remember will be the one you wore on your first date, or anniversary. Or yesterday. Instead of feeling affronted, you should feel soothed, because it proves something the fast-fashion industry would prefer to keep secret: people don't remember.

Or, fine, maybe your best friend remembers. A person who knows you and your wardrobe so intimately that you can say, 'Y'know, the green thing? I was wearing it the day we saw the dog that looked like Woody Harrelson?' and they can say, 'Of course, of course, I was with you at "green thing"!' In which case you can skip straight to reason number two, which is this:

2) They don't care. People do not care.

Think about it, and flip the scenario around. A friend or colleague or whoever turns up to meet you, and barely before you can even ask how they are, they bleat: 'I was wearing this last time I saw you, you must think I have no clothes AHAHAHAHA.' You don't think less of them, do you? Of course you don't. If anything, it makes you like them more.

No, it is the friend or colleague with the seemingly limitless conveyor belt of brand-new outfits that really rankles, because they make us feel like re-wearing our own clothes is something to be ashamed of. They're the ones exacerbating the pressure, even while we applaud them and ask them to twirl. But every time another woman stands in a fitting room, takes a deep breath and says, 'You know what? I'm just going to wear the green thing again,' we can all breathe a collective sigh of relief.

Of course, knowing logically that nobody cares if you're wearing the orange jumper again doesn't necessarily stop you feeling ashamed of it. Even without other people noticing or caring, there can be an inward compulsion to present a new and varied version of yourself to the world each time you emerge in it. That's hard to shake. I think this is especially true if you're someone who loves clothes, but who struggles to love themselves (hi). It's especially true if you're someone who gets so jazzed by the endless possibilities of fashion as a tool for self-reinvention that she pins her self-worth on it like a fancy brooch (also hi).

Still, not everyone abides by the outfit-repeating code of shame. There are alternative models, if you look for them. You know who does wear the same clothes all the time? Marge Simpson. Angela Merkel. Dame Judi Dench. Every 'effortless' French woman, being insouciant in a white shirt and trench coat.

You know who else wears the same outfit all the time? Men.

Centuries of men. Hordes of them, in their one good suit and two slightly different ties, or their crotch-worn jeans and weekend hoodie. There was a period around Christmas 2013 where my boyfriend wore the same snowman jumper every day for a full month without suffering any social repercussions whatsoever. Eventually I confiscated it, pleading hygiene and the fact it was almost March, but really I was just jealous. Imagine! Imagine caring so little. The audacity of achieving radical self-acceptance without even knowing what it is.

The luxury of not caring still isn't afforded to women in the same way, but that doesn't mean we can't claim it anyway. After all, it wasn't always like this. Your nan didn't have a new dress every time she went dancing down the palais. In 1930, the average American woman reportedly owned nine outfits.[105]

Literature from that period is a window into a time where a new frock was a rare, precious jewel, trotted out for every occasion. You'd think reading books full of girls saying things like, 'My blue taffeta will have to do for the party – I'll turn up the hem so nobody can see where it got trod on by the vicar!' might have helped temper my penchant for emergency Primark binges, but apparently not. The more choice we have, it seems, the faster we get bored. The greater the pressure to be constantly debuting new, un-vicar-sullied *lewks*. The less we get to wear the orange jumper.

And that's a shame, because we love the orange jumper. The orange jumper looks great. That's why you want to wear it, deep down. It's why whoever you're seeing today will say, 'Hey, nice orange jumper! Is it new?' and you will smile blithely and say, 'Oh, this? No, I've worn it loads. But I wouldn't expect you to remember.'

> 'Women usually love what they buy, yet hate two-thirds
> of what is in their closets.'
>
> – Mignon McLaughlin[106]

HOW TO NOT HATE ALL YOUR CLOTHES

Once you've accepted that you *do* have something to wear, the next challenge is feeling enthusiastic about those options.

Storing and caring for your clothes properly can make a big difference when it comes to not hating everything you own, but even then it's hard to fight habituation.

'Once you've been exposed to something novel a few times, you get bored of it. And that happens with clothing,' explains Dr Terrelonge. 'You go into a shop and buy a top, thinking, "It's the greatest thing, I have to have it, I love it . . ." Then you buy it, you wear it a few times maybe, you put it in the wardrobe, and months later you've forgotten about that thing you *so had* to have.'

We've internalised that need for novelty, and the stats speak for themselves: reportedly 79 per cent of women are at their happiest or most confident when wearing something new, while 52 per cent feel lacklustre or less confident when wearing something old.[107] I get this. Going back through old clothes can feel like browsing through former versions of yourself, with all their troubles and triumphs and ill-advised haircuts. Even if they're not getting physically worn out, we still tend to see them as diminishing over time; their power to make us feel good getting weaker with each passing month that they stay in our wardrobe, while the best option always exists outside in the world of the new. Fashion likes it this way. It keeps us buying more, after all.

But if the most sustainable item of clothing is the one we already own, then appreciating and wearing those clothes is one of the most powerful differences we can make. So instead of a dreary dead-end full of past mistakes and creased poly-ester, try to think of your wardrobe as though it is Narnia and a magical land of possibilities is contained within. Hopefully not ten fur coats, but that's another conversation.

This doesn't mean going back to old outfits wholesale always works. I know this because I try it all the time. You remember wearing something last year, or even last week, and feeling great – the sun was shining, your hair was shining, maybe you had a really good doughnut – and so you try to recapture that feeling by putting on the exact same clothes. But even though the clothes are the same, so many other variables are different. The weather's different, your body is different, your hair is different, your mood is different, you haven't had the doughnut. You end up feeling deflated and awkward, as though you're wearing fancy dress as your 2016 self.

No, the secret is to change just enough to make the outfit feel fresh again. Add different shoes, pair it with something from another season, use accessories to steer the outfit in a whole other direction. Challenge yourself to find new formations, before stagnation sets in. Fashion, even slow fashion, is like almond milk in coffee. *Better if you keep it moving.*

I'm sorry if all this sounds obvious, but sometimes everyone could do with a Getting Dressed refresher course. Dr Terrelonge thinks our culture of instant gratification is to blame for us losing our styling confidence; we've got so used to buying something new every time we get bored that we've forgotten we can put a jumper on over a dress. 'Because we're shopping and buying so much, people are not incorporating new pieces *into* their wardrobe,' she says. 'I think people have lost the skill to take one top and wear it different ways. They just know "that's that top and that goes with that outfit". They look at it in isolation. We shop in isolation, too . . . And because we don't know how to put things together, we think we have nothing to wear.'

Just as some people can look cool shuffling a deck of cards, it's true that some people have the knack of changing up their clothes and making it look effortless, while for the rest of us, outfit experimentation can feel awkward and stilted. But it's a skill we can all learn, and an awkwardness we can push through. The idea that style is something instinctive you 'either have or don't have' is bollocks, and it's holding us back.

Here's an embarrassing thing to admit: sometimes I make notes on people's outfits when I see them in the street. 'Scarf tied round blazer like a belt,' reads one from the other day. 'Black vest under white shirt, open, tied up,' goes another. It's nerdy as hell, but it's a proactive way to deal with a fashion inferiority complex. When I see a good outfit, instead of comparing and despairing, I take notes.

And it's through looking at other people – real, three-dimensional people – that you realise how much of a great outfit comes down to maths and science, not art. It's all about ratios. A balancing act between two opposing forces. And while we're on this scholarly trip, let's bring out GCSE English's biggest gun: juxtaposition.

Fashion loves juxtaposition. This is how throwing on a biker jacket to 'toughen up' a floaty dress became such a trope. Likewise bare legs with a chunky jumper (fashion loves temperature regulation) and throwing on a pair of trainers to dial down a smart suit (fashion also loves throwing).

You can be really quite formulaic about it. Recent + retro. Summer + winter. Floral + stripes. Silky + woolly. Posh + scuzzy. Boring + ridiculous. Salty + sweet. Something you're kinda bored of + something you still really love. If in doubt, add a contrasting layer.

Fashion also loves layers – perhaps more than anyone outside of patisserie chefs and sadistic hairdressers. You see them in the street-style photos: three coats at once and a nightie over a boiler suit. But I never understood all the fuss until I stopped shopping and had to tackle outfit ennui on a daily basis.

When you're trying to eke every last drop out of your wardrobe, layering is a game-changer. The first time you take a strappy summer dress and put it on over a long-sleeved tee, you instantly double your returns.

One of the most worn pieces of clothing in my wardrobe is a basic grey thermal poloneck from Uniqlo. I wear it under sleeveless dresses, camisoles, shirts, jumpsuits, T-shirts, chunky cardigans and floaty, slinky slips. It's a great way to downplay a dress that might otherwise be saved 'for best' (saving things 'for best' is not sustainable behaviour). And being stretchy and lightweight means no risk of feeling too 'Joey wearing all Chandler's clothes'. Everyone's biggest layering fear is doing a Joey.

By far the best advert for layering I know is my friend Caroline Jones, the slow-fashion advocate @knickers_models_own. Good layering, she tells me, is 'the bringing together of fabrics, textures, patterns, colour and shaping so that everything ties together'.

'There's always a starting point, some key elements, that might be a dress and ankle boots, or a tee and midi skirt and from there I'm looking for balance of shape and juxtaposition, always adding in something a little unpredictable.' Proving that there is no shame in working out a poindexterish process to help you get dressed in the morning, her secret weapon is the colour wheel. 'Work with two base colours or tones,' she says. 'Add a complementary colour, which could just be the gold of your jewellery or opaque coloured tights. Then work in a fourth element – it could be a punchy lip, a vivid scarf, a nail paint or a strong bangle.'

Like any style experiment, there will be layering missteps. Just now, for example, I looked down at what I thought was a breezy, 70s Californiana kind of outfit – a white shirt under a blue denim pinafore dress with ballerina flats – and realised I am in fact dressed as Belle at the beginning of Beauty and the Beast, minus the apron. But that kind of thing could happen to anyone. And you can always de-layer in the loos.

As you grow more comfortable in your own wardrobe, you get more adventurous beyond it. Caroline swears by wearing cardigans back-to-front, a trick she learned from an old issue of Jackie magazine. I've worn a dress as a top, tucked into my skirt, and a skirt as a dress, pulled up to my armpits. But you don't have to go big – sometimes a change as tiny as rolling up trouser cuffs or reverse-buttoning your shirt is all it takes to keep things feeling fresh and have friends finger-snapping at your perceptible new *vibe*.

Of course it gets much easier to not hate all of your clothes once you start buying them more thoughtfully too, and we'll get to that. But focus on the ones you have first. Love the ones you're with. Advertise the position internally before you accept outside applications.

When you think about it, habituation happens in all corners of life. The novelty wears off everything eventually – homes, relationships, babies, those Reese's Peanut Butter Eggs I bought by the fistful all last Easter – and yet we manage not to be constantly replacing and upgrading them the way we do our clothes. We take on partners, friendships, jobs, pets and homes knowing that they won't always delight us, that we might sometimes have our heads turned by other options, that they'll take a little hard work and basic maintenance to keep things ticking along.

So why not apply a little more of that commitment and stoicism to the things we own and wear? A willingness to go the distance. I take thee, grey polo neck, for warmer, for cooler, in softness and in bobbles, as long as we both shall live.

10 ways to rekindle the spark

It's always been you, baby.

1. Light candles

Candles, as we all know, are the answer to every single modern problem besides 'I spent all my money on candles'. They will create the perfect atmosphere in which to be seduced by your old clothes, plus the dim lighting means you're less likely to notice the moth holes.

2. Put on some mood music

Are there songs that remind you of your clothes? Why not make them a playlist? For example: 'Raspberry Beret' by Prince, or 'Return of the Mack' by Mark Morrison.

3. Treat them to a pampering session

Why not try washing your clothes, tenderly, by hand? Or, actually iron them for once (steamy!). Finally sew on that missing button you've had in your pocket for a year and a half. They deserve it!

4. Reminisce about good times

Remember when you were first together? Wasn't it great? Weren't you both so young and fun? Look back through old photos of the two of you together, and focus on the reasons you first fell in love. Try not to slip into a pit of post-hoc haircut regret. It's not about that right now.

5. Spend some quality time together

Plan a fun trip, just you and them. The top that seemed so boring at home might look very different paired with, say, the hills of Tuscany or the giant walrus at the Horniman Museum.

6. Take them dancing

Spend an evening grinding up against them in a basement salsa club and you might find you feel sparkier. Literally, in the case of many synthetic fibres.

7. Spice things up

Try surprising your clothes by introducing a new belt or a pair of statement earrings into the bedroom. The safe word is 'Oliver Bonas'.

8. Share your fantasies

Perhaps you've always had a secret desire to wear cheese-cloth. Maybe your clothes have always secretly longed to belong to someone who doesn't use their sleeve to mop up coffee spills. Indulging in these harmless fantasies together is a great way to recapture the magic.

9. Roleplay as strangers

Leave your clothes in a public place, such as at a bar or on a park bench, and pretend you are stumbling across them for the first time. You'll be amazed how much more exciting you find them! And if you have to tussle with a dog to get them back, even better.

10. Lend them to a friend

A little jealousy can be a powerful tool, so why not let a friend borrow your clothes? See how good they look rubbing up against someone else, and you might just find you want them back.

PART THREE: THE REBOUND

What comes next?

'My husband used to say I look at a piece of fabric and listen to the threads. It tells me a story. It sings me a song.'

– Iris Apfel[108]

SHOP 'TIL YOU STOP

I never used to understand what people meant when they said they 'hated' shopping. It always sounded deliberately contrarian, like hating dessert. Shopping was the promised land! It was how you *got more stuff!* Shopping was the route to becoming your better-dressed – and therefore better – self! What wasn't to love?

But the older I got, the more I shopped and the more The Shops refused to love me back, the more I understood.

Perhaps there's a handful of very rich, very confident people with very little else to do in life who genuinely love to shop, but for many of us it can become a strange mix of menial chore and unfulfilled fantasy, like chasing a consumer orgasm that never quite arrives.

We love the *idea* of shopping, the frivolity of it, the promise of unknown treasures out there for us to uncover. But the reality can be exhausting, physically and emotionally, pouring so much time and energy into an activity that either leaves you disappointed, or laden down with baggage you're already beginning to regret. Oh hey, like dating! I'm not reaching for these, they just keep on coming.

But, also like dating, even a savage break-up isn't enough to put you off for ever. Once the dust has settled on your split with fast fashion, once you've rediscovered your wardrobe and reprogrammed your mindset, there is a good chance you will still want to shop. Sometimes. A bit. And that's what we're going to talk about now.

Maybe we're not going to stop buying clothes for ever – but we can radically overhaul our habits to buy less, and buy better. We might even enjoy it again.

My first tip is a brutal one. If you still shop with friends on the regular, consider stopping.

Or at least, think carefully about the way your shopping partners cloud your judgement. Because even if we're not on Instagram, we are all surrounded by influencers.

When you ask a friend if you should buy something, you already know what the answer will be: yes. Unless they're one of those 'I say it like I see it people', or a good enough friend to truly have your best financial and sartorial interests at heart, they will say yes. Of course they will, because it's what we do, particularly as women. We validate each other. We enable. It's encoded, somehow, an unwritten rule of sisterhood – when another woman says, 'Should I buy this [outrageously spenny / entirely impractical / hugely uncomfortable / maybe borderline dangerous] thing?', you reply, 'YES! A THOUSAND TIMES YES!' without blinking.

If she protests, you grasp for justification. If she gives reasons not to, you shoot each one down like a profligate Annie Oakley. 'But you deserve it! But it'll look better with different shoes! But if you keep your back against the wall at all times nobody will even see the stains!' Pow, pow, pow, we hit them with excuses, until eventually they give up and buy it. Sometimes we're halfway through the routine before we realise the friend doesn't even want to buy the thing that much. It's not even that nice.

Some of the smartest shopping advice I've heard comes from Aja Barber, who tells her styling clients never to go shopping when they're feeling bad or wearing clothes they don't love. 'The easiest way to get sucked into a purchase you don't need is to go shopping in sweatpants,' she declares. 'I love sweatpants, but not in stores and I'll tell you why. If you're not wearing something which makes you feel stellar, you're more likely to take home a purchase you don't need. But when I wear my nicer clothing to go shopping, I compare what I'm trying on to what I'm already wearing. If the quality isn't a match, it doesn't go home with me.'

Just like they say you should never go food shopping hungry, it makes sense to avoid clothes shopping when you're in a low mood or a sad outfit. The temptation to fill that void with quick-fix junk is just too great. But I'm even more into Aja's idea of using our most beloved outfits to set a benchmark for all future clothes to live up to. It's a big switch in mindset, when you're used to feeling as though it is *you* that has to measure up to fashion, not the other way round – but think what a difference it would make to go shopping thinking, 'I love my clothes, so why should I buy these?' instead of, 'I hate all my clothes, must buy more.'

After all, the clothes should work hard to win us over. We should treat every shopping trip like we're Simon Cowell and clothes are *X Factor* auditionees, desperate to make it to bootcamp (bootcamp is the changing room. Judges' houses are the tills).

While popular rhetoric would have us believe that my generation is getting fussier and fussier about the way we work, the places we live and the people we date ('Why can't the youth of today just marry someone they don't love at twenty-two and work in middle management until they die?'), you could argue we've gone the opposite way with our wardrobes. Instead of waiting patiently and stubbornly for the thing that ticks all our boxes, increasingly we're prepared to settle for the thing that can be delivered tomorrow. Or to phrase it like a gift-shop fridge magnet: why keep searching for the *right* outfit when you could just have Ms Right Now?

So instead: 'Be selective, as you would select your next job, place to live or even date,' advises A Transparent Company's Neliana Fuenmayor. Or remember the immortal words of Cher Horowitz. 'You see how picky I am about my shoes, and they only go on my feet.'[109]

But even alone and with a firm handle on our own self-worth, for fashion lovers it can be hard to turn off that sense of urgency. Life is short! That's what we're told, over and over, sometimes in the same breath that warns us to slow down. Time is finite, YOLO and if we don't buy a pink corduroy safari suit *right now* then what if we die next week never having worn a pink corduroy safari suit? What if a pink corduroy safari suit was the look we should have been wearing all this time? Is it fair to deprive the world?

But just as we can't read all the books, have all the side hustles or go to all the birthday drinks, we can't wear all the trends. We just can't. We're going to need to sit a few out.

At first it might feel like a sacrifice but trust me – soon it starts to feel like a relief. Because if you allow yourself to flake out on fashion, just a bit, you free yourself from the expectation of *being fashionable.* You can eventually shake off that indefeasible feeling that no matter how hard you try and how long you shop, you'll always be slightly wrong. A bit off. Your coat won't quite be right, your hem will be two inches out, your shirt will have last season's sleeves. You'll still be wearing block heels when you're supposed to be in stiletto mules. 'Supposed to' can so easily eclipse our sense of personal style. We can lose days of our lives to 'supposed to' if we're not careful.

Once you start unpacking your relationship with shopping, it's hard to get it back in the bag. 'When I was shopping regularly, I wouldn't say I was enjoying my wardrobe at all because I was constantly seeking the next thrill,' Aja Barber admits. 'Now I'm much more aware of what I have, how to use it the most and there's a deep satisfaction there. Once I jumped off the trend boat, I felt I was truly able to find and develop myself and my style. Now it's never about having the newest thing, it's about having the best thing for ME.'

Freeing yourself from the must-shop mindset, I've found, feels like emerging from a fog. One day you look around and realise that 'everyone' isn't wearing pink corduroy safari suits at all. They're dressed in jeggings and a hoodie, or one of those jumpers with shirts sewn inside that everyone had in 2010. Except everyone didn't, because 'everyone' is an illusion.

Bust enough of these illusions and maybe we can even change how we define the word 'shop'. It's started already – bloggers call it 'shopping your wardrobe', the process of going through old clothes to see if you might want to wear some of them. At first it sounds dumbly duplicitous, like people who pretend raw dates taste like chocolate. But the more I think about it, the more I wonder if they might be on to something.

Because if shopping doesn't need to mean buying or owning, just discovering and enjoying, then we could shop as freely as we like. It could mean browsing for inspiration; what we called 'window shopping', back when we went shopping without ever expecting to buy something.

It could mean trawling your mate's wardrobes for items to borrow, perusing the virtual racks on a rental site, taking your latest dehaul to a swapping party. It could be a word that denotes a little bit of skill, creativity and flair, rather than just a debit card and directions to the nearest Zara. Shopping as a magpie, as a stylist, as someone who knows the best place to find pristine 90s streetwear or hand-painted slogan tees. An industrious person who knows which things they'll wear and love for ever, and which deserve to be left for the next person instead. Look at you, the model of self-restraint! You are *such a good shopper.*

Personally, I feel at my very shoppiest when I'm doing a charity-shop crawl. There's nothing like an afternoon spent sifting through bric-a-brac and unearthing a mega bargain from beneath a stack of Maeve Bincheys to make me feel like a champion in a way I never have scrolling ASOS, slack-jawed, on the bus.

But for you it might be different. Your shoppiest high might come from visiting some lovely independent boutique that smells of fig, just twice a year, and calmly trying on every single thing in the shop. It might be fabric shopping, flea market shopping, or a Pinterest board of runway looks from RuPaul's Drag Race. Maybe your shoppiest moment is just you, in your bedroom, playing dress-up while listening to 80s movie soundtracks.

The point is this: if shopping has ever made you feel good, trace that feeling back to the source and identify it. Work out how to do the kind of shopping you actually enjoy, and cut out the rest as far as you possibly can. Make it active, not passive. A choice, not a chore. And never be afraid to leave empty-handed.

Remember: clothes are auditioning for you, not the other way around. Don't waste your time on the ones that aren't trying hard enough.

(See also: dating.)

> *'Glamour cannot exist without personal social envy being a common and widespread emotion.'*
>
> – John Berger[110]

TREND FLU, AND HOW TO CURE IT

I write this in the summer of 2019, adrift in a sea of identical dresses. You know the one; of course you do. The Dress. It is currently everywhere, sweeping along every street and swishing ostentatiously round corners, like a polka-dot Dalek invasion.

As one of only approximately eight women in the country not to own The Dress, I could be smug about its ubiquity – except I know, if fast fashion and I were still going steady, I'd be gliding about in it with the best of them, high-fiving every other walking monochrome valance sheet to pass me in a beer garden. There should be no shame; it's a great dress. It's comfortable, breezy, it works on every body type. There but for the grace of a shopping ban go I.

And, we might add, for so many women to have honed in on this one dress from Zara, a brand that produces around 10,000 new designs a year, surely says something interesting about fast fashion.[111] Maybe we don't need or want all that choice after all. We just want one really great dress.

But fashion, as previously mentioned, is a fickle bastard, and it makes fickle bastards of us, too. I can't be the only one who has felt almost breathless with the need to buy a certain trend item before it's too late, then given it barely the tenure of a fairground goldfish. And 'too late' meaning what, exactly? Before some shadowy jury comprised of Anna Wintour, Karl Lagerfeld's cat and Lil Miquela the CGI influencer decrees it over? Or before I . . . die?

A few months ago, in the spring of my #notnewyear, as the trees flowered and the birds sang and the dog turds thawed on London pavements, The Dress was but a twinkle in Inditex's eye and instead, every second woman I saw was wearing a leopard-print midi skirt.

Most of them bought the leopard-print midi skirt towards the end of the previous summer, when leopard-print midi skirts suddenly exploded in the way basket bags had the summer before, and Aperol Spritzes had three summers before that. Trends, like germs, are more virulent in warm conditions.

All the leopard-print midi skirts looked fabulous, and I didn't have one. When they started appearing everywhere, I wanted one, a lot, but managed to talk myself out of it by reminding myself sternly that I already had a leopard-print coat, two leopard-print dresses and many midi skirts in other prints – and anyway the best ones are all bias cuts and I haven't felt good in a bias cut since 2001 (this is a whole other stern conversation, but you know how you don't always have the energy?).

Eventually, via some informal field research that involved counting pedestrians outside a branch of Itsu, I realised that it only *felt like* every second woman was wearing a leopard-print midi skirt. They weren't really; it was confirmation bias. We all do it – filtering out the inconvenient truth until we reach something that suits our agenda. We do it with climate change, and we do it with sartorial must-buys. Remember: 'everyone' is an illusion.

Of course it doesn't help that trends, like cooked spaghetti, sometimes take a few flings to stick, and it's a talent to know which ones will.

I've false-started on plenty in my time – bodysuits, silk scarves, cowboy boots – and then it's just plain frustrating, sitting around looking like a line-dancing Little Edie, waiting for everyone else to get the memo. But on the other hand, jumping on the trend train too late feels even more wasteful. If you wait too long to scratch the itch and buy that thing you've seen everywhere (military shirts, football scarves, bum bags, Dad trainers, knotted hairbands), you might only be a handful of wears away from bored and done.

Fashion often follows a rom-com pattern of revulsion and seduction. At first, you're not fussed. Maybe you think it's ugly, maybe just not your thing. But gradually, as you see more and more people wearing it and it pops up all over magazines and social feeds, it starts to grow on you. Then a fever takes hold. I like to call it 'trend flu'. One day a barely noticeable tickle, the next day a slight temperature, and then suddenly BAM! You're glassy-eyed and sweating, walking into Topshop with your arms outstretched. Pool slides, shiny vinyl, mom jeans, oversized blazers, dungarees, letterman jackets, Ukrainian peasant blouses, sheepskin coats, clogs – all strains I've succumbed to in recent years.

The best way to get over the trend flu is just to hold your nerve and ride it out. Sip fluids, rest up, eat dry crackers, don't let yourself go shopping. But if the shopping feels inevitable, there are ways to minimise the damage.

Firstly, try to find it secondhand. I know that's a challenge but trust me. The wackier the trend, the smarter it is to buy it preloved. Even if you eventually upgrade your £3 charity shop scarf or your eBay velcro sandals to a cooler, newer version, it makes sense to dip your toe in first with minimal outlay and impact. Like your parents borrowing a school saxophone until they've confirmed whether you really are the next John Coltrane/Lisa Simpson, or whether you're going to quit lessons within a term.

In the early spring of 2018, I bought a pair of tiny sunglasses in my favourite charity shop. Round pink lenses, gold rims, Kanye-approved dimension. I wore them twice. I was laughed at in the street twice. I walked into lampposts twice, because I need prescription sunglasses to actually see, and I abandoned them when it became clear that as someone who is over the age of twenty-five and not a member of the Hadid family, I was not required to participate in this trend.

On the other hand, when cowboy boots finally caught on and I had a preloved pair ready and waiting, I felt gleefully vindicated. Not my first rodeo!

Another approach, especially if you can't find the exact thing you want secondhand, is to try buying something that isn't so much on-trend as 'trend-adjacent'. So when everyone is wearing a leopard print skirt, you buy a tiger or a zebra print one. If it's white boots, get pale blue, or dig out the silver pair you probably already own. When Birkenstocks are everywhere, buy Dr Scholls instead.

Look for the lesser trends that are hovering just beneath the radar, lurking in the shadows behind The Thing That Everyone's Got. Chances are you'll end up wearing them for much longer, because if they were never at the top of the 'must-have' barometer, they can't plummet to the bottom of it either. In the same way that the highest score on a dartboard is actually at the triple twenty, not the bullseye, sometimes you score more points by aiming slightly off target.

But more importantly, also like darts, it's all just a game. Let's never forget that. Fashion is only a game, though it has the power to make losers of us all if we let it.

I'm not looking at you, Zara Dress People, when I say that. It's just that there are so many of you in my eyeline.

'I don't want more choice, I just want nicer things.'

– Edina Monsoon[112]

SHOPPING ACCORDING TO MY MOTHER

My mum has a lot of ideas about a lot of things, not least how to shop. A woman of such self-restraint that I once saw her put a tablespoonful of crumble in the fridge 'for later', she abides by a strict code of conduct. Growing up I thought it was just motherish martyrdom; now I realise she was actually a mindful shopper, long before her time.

Her golden rule is this: before you can buy something, you must name three different things *you already own* that will go with it.

It's a rule you hear repeated all the time by sustainable advocates and people making an effort to reduce, reuse and recycle. And it's just sensible, given how often 'it doesn't go with anything!' is the reason our perfectly nice clothes languish unworn. If you force yourself to identify the role a new purchase will play in your life *before* you buy it, you can keep continuity up and wild aspirations down. Remember, clothes need friends. No man is an island and no garm should be either.

If you're still dithering over a potential purchase, Mum will tell you to stick it back on the rack and go away for a few hours, then come back to see if it's still there in your size. I used to think this was about placing things in the hands of fate, but now I realise it's a cunning trick to make you step back, slow down and force a little contemplation.

If you can't stop thinking about the thing, if you'll take an elaborate detour, delay dinner or miss a train in order to go back and claim it, then you'll probably be very happy together. But if not, you can live without it and it can live without you.

At the end of the day, once our feet ached and the biscuit supply in her handbag had run out, Mum would ask if I wanted to go back and get the thing I'd been so obsessed with a few hours earlier. Sometimes I did. Sometimes it would be too much effort. Often, I'd have forgotten it even existed.

More solid tips to shop by

1. Make a note of the gaps in your wardrobe. Keep a list on your phone, or somewhere else handy, of the items you don't have right now that could facilitate the coming-together of excellent outfits or serve some other practical purpose in your life. When you do shop, it'll be easier to hone in on the gap-fillers and tune out the rest of the noise. If its name's not down, it's not coming in.

2. Go one better and operate a strict one-in-one-out policy. If any item coming into your wardrobe is going to forcibly evict an existing thing, only the hottest or most useful clothes need apply. Be the most exclusive doorkeeper you can be. Be the bouncer at Berghain.

3. Play hypotheticals. Ask yourself: if they didn't have it my size, would I be devastated? If I had to go home and buy it online instead, would I be arsed? If the till in the shop broke right now, how long would I realistically wait for them to fix it? If the answer is no, no, or less than fifteen minutes, you don't want it badly enough.

4. One of the quickest ways to assess the quality of a garment is turn it inside out and look at the seams. If they're straggly or unfinished, that's a sign that it probably won't go the distance. As sustainable fashion stylist Alice Wilby advises: 'They should look neat and tidy, not higgledy-piggledy. The closer the stitches are together, the more durable and better quality it is.'[113]

5. Remember Nora Ephron's words: 'Never marry a man you wouldn't want to be divorced from.' Each item of clothing you buy is a commitment, a thing you're responsible for in your life – even if you fall out of love eventually. So if you can't face the hassle of selling it, donating it or otherwise dealing with it after you break up with it, probably don't buy it in the first place.

> *'The fashion industry was built on secrecy and elitism;*
> *it was opaque. Transparency is disruptive – in that sense,*
> *it's a breath of fresh air and a useful weapon of change.'*

> – Orsola de Castro, Fashion Revolution[114]

IT'S NOT EASY BEING GREENWASHED

But where? That's the logical next question, isn't it? Where do we shop now? How do we work out which brands deserve our money, and which doors we should never darken again?

The answer, or at least the means to get to the answer, is transparency.

In a notoriously secretive industry, the first step is getting brands to air their laundry in public – no matter how dirty. We need them to publish their supply chains, details of their factories, where their fabric and materials are sourced from and how they're produced. We need to know how much they pay their workers, whether they recognise their right to unionise and how regularly factories are audited to check it isn't just a pack of lies. We need all the info we can get, in a place that the average customer can find it, and in language we can understand. And not just customers; the garment workers need that information, so they can negotiate for better treatment. Brands themselves could benefit too, by sharing knowledge on scientific advancements and better ways to work. As Levi's head of global product innovation, Paul Dillinger, puts it, 'If you figure out how to save water and you don't tell people about it, you're kind of a jerk.'

'Transparency is the founding ethos of Fashion Revolution,' says Bronwyn Seier, the organisation's assistant graphic designer and co-producer of sustainable design podcast *The Drop*. The most upfront brand doesn't necessarily equal the most sustainable, she explains, but 'if the information is not there, that's just a red flag straight away'. If they're not telling you proudly about the provenance of your clothes, it's because they don't want you to know – or because they don't know themselves.

Every year, Fashion Revolution publishes its Fashion Transparency Index, an assessment of the biggest global fashion brands that takes into account the information each company discloses about its suppliers, supply chain policies and the social and environmental impact of its business. Brands are ranked in five areas – Policy & Commitments, Governance, Traceability, Know, Show & Fix, and Spotlight Issues – and ranked overall. In 2019, the average score across all 200 brands was 21 per cent, which sounds dismal, but that was a 5 per cent increase across the brands reviewed the year before, and a 9 per cent increase on brands reviewed the year before that.[115] No major brands scored above 70 per cent in 2019, but that's an improvement on 2018 when none scored above 60 per cent, and 2017 when none scored above 50 per cent. Steadily, brands are stepping up to be held accountable, as more and more shoppers demand to know the full story.

Still, it can be hard to sort the sustainable pioneers from the good PR. Nearly all savvy fashion retailers these days will have some kind of ethical bumf on their website – often nebulous, often next to useless. 'Commitments' and 'promises', more dubious pledges than a fraternity house, Corporate Social Responsibility (CSR) statements full of incomprehensible legalese. Boasts of a 'zero-tolerance approach', as though being against modern slavery is a stance to be applauded, rather than just base-level human decency.

Known as greenwashing, this kind of tricksy marketing is on the rise, as companies put more effort into pulling the wool over our eyes than they do into creating real change. It's no surprise that of the five sections in the Fashion Transparency Index, 'Policy & Commitments' has by far the highest average score (a still-not-amazing 48 per cent)[116] – after all, it's easy to make promises, and draw up nice, clean codes of conduct using a team of pricey lawyers. It's much harder for brands to pull their fingers out and do the messy work of enforcing them.

Take H&M. Often cited as one of the cleanest, greenest options on the high street, the brand ranks near the top of the Fashion Transparency Index with a score of 61 per cent.[117] It was one of the first to launch a dedicated eco-conscious line, one of the first to make its supplier list public, and has vowed that all its cotton will be organic, recycled or sourced through the Better Cotton Initiative by 2020.[118] In short, it spins a nice yarn.

Back in November 2013, the H&M group (which has a stable of nearly 5,000 stores worldwide, including H&M, Monki, Cos, Weekday, Arket and & Other Stories) announced, to much media fanfare, that all of its strategic suppliers 'should have pay structures in place to pay a fair living wage by 2018', an advance that they estimated would benefit around 850,000 textile workers.[119] And yet when 2018 arrived, the Clean Clothes Campaign spoke to the company's garment workers in Bulgaria, Turkey, India and Cambodia and found that none of them was earning anywhere near a living wage. Not even half. In Bulgaria, workers were earning just 10 per cent of a living wage, despite working eighty-hour weeks.[120]

H&M responded by holding a 'fair wage summit' and commissioning an independent review of its 'roadmap' for wages. 'What we have learned from our experiences, we will bring with us in our future work,' insisted the company's global sustainability manager, Jenny Fagerlin.

Even among smaller brands, greenwashing can be a problem. All those new indie labels creeping into our Insta feed to seduce us with tanned shoulders, shirred gingham and aphorisms about integrity in nice cursive script. There are brands who base their whole sales pitch around being sweatshop-free, without ever explaining where their clothes are produced or who by. They might boast about 'natural fibres' without acknowledging that cotton is a problematic fave, or mention a friendly team of 'in-house designers', as though it's magically impossible to use factories in Bangladesh if you also have an office in Somerset.

Of course, none of this is to say that a brand has to be 100 per cent perfect before we buy from them, or that we can't applaud good intentions. These small brands probably *are* a more sustainable option, all things considered – but if they don't explain why or how, then we can't know for sure. You know what they say about assuming and asses.

So how do we decode the spiel and find out the facts, without it becoming a full-time research job? Obviously, there's an app for that.

Good On You (goodonyou.eco) is currently the world's leading source for fashion sustainability ratings. Led by campaigners, scientists, academics and industry insiders, the Good On You directory features 2,200 brands at the time of writing, all rated by a five-point system that takes into account more than fifty different certification schemes and standards. Child labour, modern slavery, worker safety, living wages, energy use, carbon emissions, water consumption, chemical waste, animal welfare – it's all represented.

And it's a good thing Good On You is so thorough, because otherwise we might be tempted to turn a blind eye to curve balls like this: Boden is rated lower than Primark.

Genuinely. Or: Warehouse scores 0 out of 5 on People, Planet *and* Animals. I know! And yet they do such lovely florals! To spend an evening playing on the directory is to step through the looking glass and not be able to go back. Before you know it, it's 2am and you're still sat there, typing in every brand you can think of and reeling at the results.

But if the information isn't there either, we can do a little extra homework. We can reach out and ask for it.

#WhoMadeMyClothes has been the rallying cry of Fashion Revolution since 2013, and every year it's got louder. The hashtag receives millions of impressions every April, 720 million in 2018, as more people in more countries use it to post a 'label selfie' and ask brands for transparency.[121] Plenty still falls on deaf ears, but by the end of 2018, some 3,838 companies had responded – and with them, makers proclaiming #IMadeYourClothes, and farmers saying #IMadeYourFibre.[122]

Fashion Revolution even has an email template online, so we can ask #WhoMadeMyClothes at the click of a button.[123] 'It might not be that they'll give you a clear answer,' says Seier, 'but the more people they have asking those questions, the more they will address it.'

We can't be afraid to ask more, and expect more from the companies who want to clothe us. This is not a time for our would-you-minds and sorry-to-bother-you-buts. Think of all the money you've given those brands in the past, and all the money you might be prepared to give them in the future. Then go and quiz them like a precocious child. Where? How? Who? Whyyyy?

A four-word question might seem like scant action to tackle a problem as knotty and complicated as fast fashion, but it plants a seed that lays down roots and opens up conversations. Eventually, if we keep asking, transparent will become the new opaque. Pressure equals progress.

'What is ethical fashion? It's a confusing term. Sometimes it's easier to define by what it isn't – and unfortunately that is most of what can be found on the high street.'

– Safia Minney, founder of People Tree[124]

FAST AND HIGH

By the way – when I say 'fast fashion' I don't necessarily mean 'the high street' or vice versa. It's a hazy distinction I know, but they're not completely interchangeable.

In this break-up, the high street is more like the ex's loyal gang of mates. You probably won't see most of them again, because it's too awkward and they're positioned too far behind enemy lines. But that isn't to say one or two good eggs won't survive the cull and become semi-regular 'let's go for a drink, it's been ages!' pals. Your 'Marks & Spencer friends', if you will.

Marks & Sparks might be flailing, but in sustainability terms it's flying higher than most of the high street just now, making significant strides in its efforts to phase out hazardous chemicals, minimise plastic, audit working conditions and reward shoppers for recycling unworn clothes.[125] And it seems important to say this somewhere so I may as well say it now: I don't want M&S to die, any more than I want the Queen or the BBC or McVitie's biscuits to die.

While every sustainability advocate has their own idea of an ideal future, I don't think many of them *want* huge job losses, empty shops or beloved stores crashing and burning as we all abandon the high street in our droves to stay home and darn. I know I certainly don't. And the brands we feel loyal to are in a far better position than the ones we feel borderline masochistic about, because we will root for them to improve instead of cutting them off cold turkey. We want them to do better, and be better, and make us feel better too.

But just like @RoyalFamily, iPlayer or the launch of the gluten-free Hobnob, cultural institutions have to evolve. They have to keep winning us over, again and again, changing their game plan as customers change theirs and giving us new reasons to stay loyal to our old favourites. If M&S (and John Lewis, Clarks, all those guys) can give us the slow fashion the world needs, they can keep their national-treasure status and I can keep buying my favourite knickers. Here's hoping.

'One day we'll wake up and Green will not be the new black, it will be the new invisible. Meaning, no longer will sustainable be the exception or something that's considered au courant; instead it will be a matter of course'

– Summer Rayne Oakes[126]

SUSTAINABLE FASHION IS MORE THAN JUST SACK DRESSES
(but there are still quite a lot of sack dresses)

Close your eyes and think about the phrase 'ethical fashion'. What visuals spring to mind?

I'll start: there is linen. There are scarves. There are scratchy utility fabrics and flowy jersey 'basics'. There are dropped crotches, tunics, elasticated waistbands, dresses that go out where they should go in and in where they should go out. Trousers designed purposely to make one's arse look like a potato in a paper bag. There is khaki, and grey, and a veritable rainbow of beige, extending from millet to lentil through a spectrum encompassing every kind of ancient grain.

There are prints too: the 'National Trust tea towel' kind, the 'loved by white ladies who once went to Kerala' kind, and, more recently, the 'whichever way you squint at this abstract squiggle, it will reveal itself to be a vulva' kind. You might even be able to smell certain smells – alfalfa sprouts, tobacco flower, hessian sacking, feet – or hear the distant clink of a wind chime. Perhaps you're feeling panicky by association, as though a chatty woman in an empty boutique is about to make you spend £30 on a handbag made from cork. You might notice the first twinges of an IBS episode, from all the ancient grains. It's okay, you can unclench. This is a safe space. Breathe.

The great news is that we're wrong – or at least, not wholly right. Conscious fashion has come a long way, baby.

While for a long time the porridgey smock dress reigned supreme, the last few years have brought with it a boom in genuinely stylish, inventive labels doing their bit to bridge the gap between fast fashion's sugar rush and ethical fashion's slow-release energy. Which is nice, because while it makes sense that some conscious consumers would like their clothes to represent a rejection of 'fashion' in every respect, others of us would still like to show the world our style. And our waists.

In 2018, fashion site Lyst reported a 47 per cent increase in shoppers looking for items with terms such as 'vegan leather' and 'organic cotton'.[127] And as the number of customers asking 'who made my clothes?' and 'how?' rises, so does the number of young designers and entrepreneurs determined to do things differently. Not just 'in spirit' (everyone's doing it differently in spirit) but in solid, traceable supply chains and quantifiably cleaner production. Frustratingly there is still no one agreed definition for 'sustainable' or 'ethical' fashion – it's up to shoppers to draw our own conclusions – but increasingly there's no one look, either.

Founded in 1991, People Tree has long been held up as an example of ethical fashion done right. Fairtrade certified, the global womenswear brand uses organic and Fairtrade cotton, TENCEL™ and other eco-friendly fabrics, and their clothes are made by small groups of artisans in developing countries, all of which are clearly listed and regularly vetted by the company. They're nice clothes, too – if still quite determinedly in the 'is it an outfit or is it pyjamas?' realm. Emma Watson's a fan.

But if you aren't, there's an ever-diversifying rollcall of indie labels to discover. Brands who are designing out waste, putting sustainability at the heart of their business model and striving to make a positive impact, rather than just minimising the bad. Like Amy Powney's Mother of Pearl, the luxury womenswear line with high-fashion aesthetic but low-impact production. Like Kemi Telford, whose voluminous cotton silhouettes look bang-on trend but are made to last decades. Like Veja, whose fairtrade vegan sneakers are suddenly everywhere, including on Meghan Markle's feet. Mayamiko, whose colourful vegan collections are made in Malawi by a cooperative of women who source local fabrics to minimise their carbon footprint. E.L.V. Denim, which patches together pieces of old discarded jeans to create entirely new, unique pairs with a featherlight environmental footprint.

Lucy & Yak, whose organic cotton dungarees have a well-deserved cult following. Mary Benson, who makes her glam rock prairie dresses to order, so there's never any waste. The Knotty Ones, which sells gorgeous knitwear made by stay-at-home mums in Lithuania. I could go on, and I will.

There's Sancho's, the chic Exeter-based boutique which in 2020 began trialling a transparent pricing system that allows customers to pay what they can afford. Vana, whose loafers and ballet flats are made from cruelty-free alpaca wool with 100 per cent recycled soles. Studio One Eighty Nine, whose scene-stealing designs are made by artisanal communities in Ghana. Community Clothing, designer Patrick Grant's social enterprise, which utilises the quiet periods at Lancashire textile factories to produce sustainable staples and keep the factories in business. Rakha, which makes incredibly stylish button-down skirts and blouses using recycled vegan fabric and seashells. Lara Intimates, which makes very cool lingerie from reclaimed fabric offcuts. People, the award-winning Birmingham brand with a nice line in slouchy jumpsuits and crisp linen. Hades Knitwear, whose art and punk-inspired pure wool sweaters are all handmade in Scotland. Rapanui, which makes slogan tees as sustainable as they are genuinely desirable. Swimwear brands Deakin & Blue and Batoko, whose ECONYL swimsuits – made from regenerated ocean waste – are fast becoming a feature at every lido in the country.

Then there are the online boutiques collating and evaluating them all, so we don't have to. Mamoq, Know The Origin, Gather & See . . . I'll stop now, because you know how to type 'ethical fashion brands' into Google. And you should.

However, there's still a long old way to go before we all buy new clothes sustainably as standard. And I think a lot of that is down to attitude; theirs as well as ours.

Even now, at a time when new ethical fashion labels are sprouting all over the place, it's easy to flick through a few websites and conclude that sustainable fashion is little more than a smug circle-jerk for lithe yoga instructors who would look chic in a hospital gown. The same adjectives abound – 'cool', 'understated', 'androgynous', 'simple', 'timeless'. But clothes that feel flamboyant, sassy, flirty, outlandish, camp, disco-fabulous or unabashedly feminine are still harder to find.

Look, I understand that there are practical and logistical reasons ethical clothes can't look exactly the same as the ones in Zara . . . but I also kind of don't. If the food scientists can make vegan burgers that bleed, surely the ethical fashion pioneers should be able to give us the clothes we really want to wear? *Ethically.*

'There's certainly a misconception that [sustainable fashion] is boring but, honestly, I don't think that's helped by the never-ending supply of brands creating truly boring "sustainable staples",' admits journalist Sophie Benson, who spends her days researching and writing about the topic.

Although she does add, loyally, that 'the boundaries that sustainable fashion put up can be a creative challenge and an opportunity to check out of the fashion cycle and cultivate a style that's truly yours.'

It's not just a question of taste. The world of sustainable fashion replicates the same inequalities found more broadly in fashion as a whole.

'It's rich that sustainable fashion brands can voice such opinions when 95 per cent of them only make clothes up to a size 14/16. How can a brand be that fashion-forward if they don't cater for the majority of the population?' demands Grace Victory when I raise the topic. That isn't a real stat, but it feels true. In every documentary I have watched and every article I have read, almost all of these pioneering ethical and sustainable fashion entrepreneurs, these inspirational, motivational women in their chic organic cotton, have been thin. Most have been white.

Aja Barber puts it plainly: 'The sustainable fashion movement is at risk of being elitist, exclusionary and, I'll add, riddled with white supremacy,' she says. 'All these movements, whether it's homesteading or zero waste, should have people of colour at the front and yet the sustainable movement that we see on Instagram is entirely too whitewashed for my liking.'

And the further away we are from that narrow fashion 'ideal', the harder it can be to feel enthusiastic about quitting fast fashion. After all, while most of the mainstream fashion industry has pussyfooted around inclusivity for years, some of the fastest brands have blazed the brightest trail. Boohoo, Missguided and ASOS often create the most racially diverse and the least tokenistic campaigns. Models with stretchmarks, scars, birthmarks and skin conditions have all graced their sites and billboards looking fierce and fashionable. Tall, petite and plus-size options are far easier to find in fast fashion than their 'conscious' counterparts, and bigger models have become a more standard part of their advertising, rather than a special gimmick.

'We've taken a bodycon dress and put it on a size 10 model next to a size 20,' Boohoo co-founder Carol Kane has stated.[128] I suppose this is supposed to sound impressive.

Diverse marketing and inclusive sizing are no excuse for terrible labour practices or environmental damage, but they're a valid reason many shoppers still want to buy from those brands. To feel seen, and celebrated. The responsible labels could take note. Especially the self-declared 'thoughtful' brand I saw last year recommending a particularly dreamy dress 'for smaller busts' because it 'can't be worn with a bra'. *So thoughtful!*

One designer hoping to change all this is Jazmin Lee, who launched indie plus-size brand Plus Equals in a bid to give consumers the colourful, expressive fashion she'd always wanted for herself. 'I feel that we are often left behind,' she tells me. 'I think this boils down to structural fatphobia and how we, as fat bodies, are seen by the ethical markets – we are seen as greedy, over-consumers, gluttonous and we should simply just "wait until we have lost weight" to be able to buy.'

Lee's clothes are a million miles from a hemp muumuu; they're riotous, sequinned, skintight and rainbow bright. The whole range is non-binary, available in sizes 14–42 (and made to measure above a size 42), and all handmade by Lee herself. Equally cheering is Loud Bodies, a Romanian-based label founded by twenty-three-year-old Patricia Luiza Blaj, whose designs run from XXS to 5XL. A parade of prairie ruffles, fluted sleeves, plunging wraps and pussy bows, they provide happy proof that it's possible to create inclusive, sustainable clothes that are also what my gran would call 'in the fashion'.

But Lee is still pragmatic about fashion's size problem. 'I get both ends of the scale. As someone who has set up a small business, it is impossible to stock ranges that cater for everyone unless you have a large-scale budget,' she says. 'On the other hand, you have many businesses that *do* and *can* make to order, and have plus-size shoppers crying out to buy their items.'

With all this going on, deciding where to spend your money can start to feel like a Milkshake Duck.[129] Here's a feminist T-shirt raising funds for charity! Oh wait, it was made in a sweatshop. Here's a brand making strides to champion diversity! Oh wait, every single one of their executives is a white man named Steve. Here's a – oh wait, never mind. Cancelled. Shut it down.

No company can be perfect, and certainly not overnight. But the most sustainable brands are the ones that respect both the people making their clothes, and the people they're selling them to.

Let's not forget the notorious American Apparel, once applauded for manufacturing its retro-tinged athleisurewear 'ethically' in its LA factory, while also relying on hyper-sexualised marketing with an inescapable male gaze. When a string of sexual harassment lawsuits were filed against its founder, Dov Charney, it felt like going back to square one again. The Milkshake Duck with a hipster moustache.

But good stuff comes out of bad, and one good thing was Birdsong London. Co-founder Sophie Slater was once an American Apparel employee. 'I hated the way they marketed to women and I hated the way they treated women,' she says. She became determined to prove that truly sustainable fashion *is* feminist fashion, and vice versa.

The company was borne out of activism but filtered through an unapologetic love of clothes. Birdsong works with groups of female artisans, all paid a living wage, while the brand's motto, 'no sweatshops, no Photoshop' strives to make sure its visuals are every bit as empowering as its production. Birdsong isn't perfect either, Sophie insists, but they welcome criticism. 'I think if you're getting called out, people care enough to engage, so it's a really good sign. And it gives you the chance to improve.'

So if we can't find the clothes we want to buy with the values we want to invest in, we can make noise. Badger the brands we love to do better, and help 'better' brands understand where they're going wrong. We can't be afraid to say we don't want to wear the sack dresses, if we don't want to wear the sack dresses. Sustainable fashion should be able to sustain a two-way conversation. It can't be the guy at the party who bellows about his charity work while eating all of the hummus. Nobody likes that guy.

Or as Stella McCartney puts it: 'You can't ask a consumer to compromise. I don't think you can say, "Here is this jacket that looks terrible but it's organic, and here is a really beautiful jacket that's cheaper but don't buy it because it's not organic."'[130] Stella gets it. Which is fabulous for people who can afford her clothes.

But while having the time, money and knowledge to shop sustainably is a privilege, it's also a mistake to think that only the bougie elite are prepared to pay for ethical brands. A 2015 study in the US found sustainability sentiment 'is particularly consistent across income levels', with those earning $20,000 or less actually 5 per cent *more* willing than those earning over $50,000 to pay more for products from companies committed to positive social and environmental impact.[131] Being skint doesn't mean we stop caring. If anything, it can make us more determined to use the money we do have in the most positive way we can.

Either that, or rich people have no soul. It's hard to say.

'There needs to be more representation of people discussing sustainability: when it's a reserved platform of the wealthy, it is hard to filter down,' says *The Frugality*'s Alex Stedman. 'In fact, the very idea of no waste and reusing everything ten times is something my working-class nan swore by, and whose values I try and keep with me as much as possible.'

Which is another good point: we can't call clothes sustainable if they're not durable too. Especially if we're buying on a budget – we need to know it's going to go the distance and not need replacing after a couple of washes. We need things nan-approved.

Luckily there are labels looking way past the #30Wears mark. Entrepreneur Tom Cridland invented his 30 Year Sweatshirt after watching *The True Cost*, and has since expanded into a whole collection of clothes backed by three-decade guarantees. If they shrink, tear or wear out within thirty years, customers can send them back for free repairs. Activist adventurewear brand Patagonia offers an 'Ironclad Guarantee' on all its clothes, with free repairs on items that don't perform as promised. MUD Jeans offers a free repairs service too, as well as a 'lease' model with a small monthly fee that gives customers the option to send back their jeans after twelve months to exchange them for a brand-new pair. The returned jeans are then recycled into new ones and sold again.

One MUD stockist is Siobhan Wilson, owner of Brighton boutique The FAIR Shop. 'People perceive that sustainable fashion is more expensive but we have actually had customers say that they save money by shopping sustainably,' she says. 'It's about buying less and choosing things that you really love and will want to take care of and keep for as long as possible.' Because the smallest members of society often grow out of clothes before they have a chance to wear them out, The FAIR Shop also takes part in a Smarter Uniforms initiative which kits out kids with secondhand school clothes for a third of the original price – a lifeline for many parents when you consider that the average spend on each school uniform is £160 per child.[132] 'Shops at their best are places for the community,' says Wilson.

And there's another reason to give sustainable shops a chance. With a change in ethos on one side of the counter comes a change in experience on the other. Even if we think we're done with the high street, full stop, the new breed of free-range boutique can offer so much more than just clothes and trinkets. They're often education hubs and arts spaces, hosting talks and workshops and spearheading local campaigns. They'll teach you to glaze a pot with one hand while eating a vegan blondie with the other. If you're confused about the many, many facets of sustainability, they're the place to take your questions (not my inbox, just so we're clear). It's easy to forget when you're used to homogenous chain stores, but a shop can also be a place to stop and chat.

In the future, 'sustainable' won't have a personal style. There will be sustainable brands for goths and vamps, anarchists and basic bitches alike. We'll be able to do princessy glamour just as ethically as high-concept androgyny, and we'll all be able to afford it and fit into it all and wear it all for decades. There'll be sustainable clothes that do look like Zara, and maybe even a Zara that's legitimately sustainable. After all,

Inditex recently pledged that by 2025, 100 per cent of its fabric will be from sustainable sources.[133] We can dream.

In the meantime, the options are looking better, brighter and less like a mung bean salad with each passing month. Sometimes, I suppose, you just need a bit of roughage to get things moving.

Material values

Five exciting fabrics to look out for.

1. Piñatex

This vegan alternative to leather is made from pineapple leaves, which would normally end up burned or discarded. Unlike PVC 'cruelty-free' leather, which is toxic both to make and discard, Piñatex is biodegradable, waste-reducing, and allows pineapple farmers in the Philippines to earn extra income on their crops. It's less expensive than real leather too, with a pleasingly distressed finish that will save you years of 'breaking in' time.

2. TENCEL™

The brand name for lyocell or modal fibres, TENCEL™ is made from wood pulp, like viscose, and shares the same smooth, slippy properties. But unlike most viscose, it uses trees from sustainably managed plantations and a closed-loop method in which solvents are recycled again and again with as little as 1 per cent wasted. TENCEL™ uses less water to produce than cotton, and is 50 per cent more absorbent too, making it ideal for sportswear or any other potentially sweaty situations.

3. ECONYL

Currently making a splash in the swimwear world, ECONYL is going to great lengths to help solve the problem of ocean pollution. The regenerated nylon is made from fishing nets and industrial plastic waste dredged up from oceans and landfill around the world, and its inventors claim it can be infinitely recycled without losing quality or purity.

4. Cupro

A vegan alternative to silk with the same luxury feel, Cupro is made from linter, a by-product of cotton that would normally be wasted. Manufactured in a closed-loop system, which means the chemicals and wastewater used in its production are reused again and again, it's also biodegradable, easily recycled and machine-washable. 'Dry clean only' can do one.

5. Hemp

Marijuana's sober cousin is out to redeem its dreary sandal-wearing reputation. Requiring no pesticides, very little water and comparatively small amounts of land to grow, there's no doubt as to hemp's environmental credentials – but its style kudos is looking up too. New, refined production means the days of rough hessian textures are over, and there are countless brands using it to make clothes that are more hip, less hippie. Inhale at leisure.

PS

Remember single-fibre fabrics are far easier to recycle than mixed fibres, so it's better to choose 100 per cent silk, 100 per cent cotton or even 100 per cent polyester over fabric blends. But if you fall in love with a mongrel, that's okay – just be prepared to love it, keep it, or pass it on in one piece.

> *'Happiness quite unshared can scarcely be called happiness;*
> *it has no taste.'*
>
> – Charlotte Brontë[134]

SWAP, SHARE, RENT, REPEAT

It is my dream that one day, in the future, a free public lending library will exist for wedding outfits.

Never again will we waste good money on things we'd never wear outside of a Cotswolds marquee, like pastel boleros or nude slingback heels. We'll simply log our brief ('barn, June, jazz band, must have ample room for hog roast') in the app and then choose from a plethora of free outfits, which we will receive via courier two days before the wedding and return two days later for the next lucky guest ('humanist, July, vegan buffet, must not upstage bridal culottes'). The whole thing would be paid for by our taxes because it would provide a vital service, both in environmental terms and for the sanity of its users.

Grassroots versions of this model are happening already, all the time. In WhatsApp groups, offices, flatshares, anywhere else people assemble to wail 'what the hell can I weeeeeear' while others helpfully proffer clutch bags and pashminas.

Instead of shelling out for a new outfit knowing we might only wear it once ('church, October, cèilidh, must intimidate ex's new girlfriend in incredibly classy way'), imagine if we all joined forces. Imagine all the things we could accomplish if we weren't eternally shopping for weddings.

Not just weddings. Funerals. Holidays. Saturday nights. Maternity wear. Wetsuits. There are so many clothes that we only need for micro-periods of time and then never again; if we pooled our collected resources and shared them out in an organised fashion, think of the difference it could make to our fashion footprint, our wardrobe space, and our lives.

But until my state-sponsored free-for-all dream comes true, there's the next best thing: rental.

Formal gown hire has been around for ages, of course. In my home town, the stately Carolyn Keyes Dress Design has been hiring out prom dresses since before UK proms were even a thing. Designer rental sites Girl Meets Dress and Rent The Runway have both been in the game since 2009 – the latter now valued at an eye-watering $1 billion[135] – and more recently they've been joined by a handful of similarly luxe high-fashion hire brands aimed at wedding-goers and fashion-week frow-ers. Oprent, Front Row, Wear The Walk. The latter operates on a system of 'credits' not unlike an amusement arcade, but instead of a pound for three goes on a dance mat, it's £149 for a go on a directional jumpsuit.

Yet only very recently has clothes rental started to become an everyday option, rather than a Cinderella fantasy. In the US, Urban Outfitters launched its own rental platform,

Nuuly, in the summer of 2019. Meanwhile, on this side of the pond there's a new generation of startups more focused on sustainability than sequins, keen to turn our 'must-haves' into must-borrows.

One is Onloan, the fashion subscription service co-founded by Natalie Hasseck and Tamsin Chislett. 'On average, customers lose that exciting "new" feeling after a month,' explains Hasseck. 'On subscription you can experience that new feeling month on month – without the guilt.' One of the company's core beliefs is that 'the dopamine hit comes from the thrill of discovering and wearing new clothes, not the ownership of them'.

Rather than renting individual items, Onloan sends you a regular delivery of clothes to wear for a month, then return. After the clothes are taken out of circulation, they're sold on, with subscribers getting first dibs. Stock is curated from hip indie brands like ALEXACHUNG, By Malene Birger, House of Dagmar, Kitri and Mykke Hofmann, and can be rented at a monthly rate of £79 for two pieces, £109 for three pieces and £169 for five – which might sound like a big outlay for a month's wear, but then you could say the same for so many impulse purchases. 'We've priced our subscription packages to compete with an average "accidental high-street spend',"' says Hasseck. 'That last minute dash to & Other Stories – it's super easy to drop £80–£100 on two or three items.' Guilty as charged.

'For me, the rental revolution is the future of fashion,' says Victoria Prew, co-founder of HURR Collective, the UK's first peer-to-peer rental platform. She predicts that within a couple of years, we'll all be at it. 'You will have a box of clothes on a Monday morning that turns up to your house and you will wear them for a week or a couple of weeks, and that is how we will all consume fashion.'

Unlike traditional hire companies which buy their own stock, HURR operates as a kind of Airbnb for fashion. Users can list their clothes on the site, use geotagging to find the best pieces near them, and meet up in public places to exchange the goods. It's the personal and social connection of clothes-swapping, but with a price tag for your trouble.

While weddings and 'events' are as popular as you'd expect, the number-one reason for renting on HURR is holidays. Which makes sense these days, when a package deal to the Algarve can feel like a week-long photo op. Why buy the Cult Gaia bamboo handbag or the Castañer espadrilles when you can rent them for a weekend, get the perfect Insta snap and give someone else the bother of shaking the sand out?

Something the new generation of fashion-rental companies all have in common is a willingness to meet customers in the middle, reflecting our real-life habits while still prioritising sustainability. Trends aren't off the menu – they're to be enjoyed, celebrated, and then passed on to the next person. Both HURR and Onloan say their ethos is about encouraging customers to build an everyday capsule wardrobe of high-quality, sustainably-made basics – jeans, T-shirts, coats, trainers – and then rent the rest. When ethical fashion starts to feel like a diet of brown rice and beans, clothes rental adds a fresh punch of flavour.

'What we want is to be able to give people access, rather than ownership,' Prew tells me. 'Millennials that pride access over owning things can access amazing designer pieces that they might otherwise not be able to afford, wear them once or twice and then send them back. It's a really clever way, I think, to democratise the designer fashion market.' Albeit a democracy with a waitlist. Within three months of its launch, HURR had a queue of more than 2,000 eager users keen to sign up.

But still, it's a great sign that we might be ready to start sharing – and that there are thousands of wardrobes out there, ripe for the rummage. If the most sustainable clothes are the ones already in your wardrobe, then the second most sustainable are the clothes in somebody else's.

That's the philosophy behind the Leeds Community Clothes Exchange, one of the UK's many clothes-swapping events. Founded by a group of friends in 2008, the Exchange has been running for an impressive 11 years and now holds volunteer-run events on a near-monthly basis.

'It was the norm when I was a child to pass on clothes to friends and family, but at some point it developed a stigma as something "poor" people did; people wanted to buy new instead – which the fast-fashion retailers helped to facilitate,' says LCCE organiser Lauren Cowdery, who gave up high-street shopping for good four years ago. 'There are still lots of people who are hung up on hoarding their clothes. Clothes that don't fit which they plan to "slim into", expensive items they don't want to part with even though they don't wear them, sentimental items . . . it's not always a bad thing, but I think if it doesn't fit or you can't or won't wear it, it's better to pass it on for someone else to enjoy,' she says.

The term 'swishing' was coined by sustainable communications agency Futerra in 2007, as part of an effort to organise clothes-swapping events on a nationwide scale. Similar projects and initiatives are popping up all the time, with different names and rules but the same general idea: you turn up with your clothes (in wearable condition only) and exchange them for credits. Sometimes there's a small entrance fee. Then you 'shop' everyone else's items. Often there'll be half an hour for browsing at the beginning, to minimise panic and fisticuffs. And at LCCE events, credits even carry over on members' accounts until the next month, so there's no pressure to take home just any old tat.

Not that you're obliged to be sensible either. Cowdery tells me that clothes-swapping has made her style much more experimental. 'I think one of the perceptions that puts people off slow fashion is that they'll have to spend a large amount of money on a "classic" item,' she says. 'But you can certainly be a fashion magpie sustainably. Swapping is great for this, as you can try out an outfit or style without having to commit money to it, and can pass it on easily if it doesn't work for you.'

Clothes swapping is hardly a niche idea, or a very new one. Back in 2013, the ladies of Ambridge even held a swishing party on *The Archers* to raise money for the organ fund. But if there was previously a faint tinge of Tupperware party or Avon catalogue about the whole thing – you know, the unfounded fear you'll be cajoled into a cardigan with a cat motif so as not to insult someone's aunt – then that's definitely on the way out. As part of their project Stories Behind Things, perennially cool sustainability influencers Jemma Finch and Ella Grace Denton run The Big Clothes Switch in London on a bi-monthly basis, complete with 'wellness market', while Depop has hosted characteristically hip swap shops in Bristol, Edinburgh and Liverpool.

Even if the idea of a hall full of strangers sifting through our cast-offs makes us shudder, it's hard to deny that sharing clothes makes sense on every score: financially, ecologically, even romantically. We can still swap and share on a smaller scale, and reap the rewards.

Perhaps it's because I never had a sister, but I've always been genuinely thrilled when friends want to raid my wardrobe. Clothes are the currency of my affection. Like a grandma filling your pockets with biscuits, I rarely let people leave my flat without pushing something on them from my heap of must-donates and should-wear-mores. I'm not fussed if they wash it or iron it or drip ice cream down the front, but I do lend with one strict proviso: all credit to me. If anyone compliments them while wearing the thing, they are obliged to yell, 'THANK YOU, IT IS LAUREN'S.'

My golden era as wardrobe mistress was my student house. Five of us lived in a falling-apart Victorian maisonette with all the makings of quality anecdotes: a bathroom you could only access through the kitchen, a virulent strain of orange mould, a highly dangerous square of flat asphalt we referred to as 'the roof terrace' and, on the roof terrace, a jar full of something unidentifiable that we simply called 'the jar'. The years I spent there were defined by shared experiences – communal hangovers, communal colds, communal boxes of doner meat and chips – and, for a while, a communal dress.

It was cobalt blue with a loud floral print. I bought it, but two of my housemates wore it as often as I did. It was all very Sisterhood of the Travelling etc, despite never really travelling further than Kilburn High Road. Everyone magically looked great in that dress.

In old photos from around 2008, any one of us might be wearing it. Sometimes it appeared on multiple people in the same Facebook album ('Weekend lolfest vol. 5!!'). One time I bumped into one of the others around campus and noticed she was clutching her coat closed, sheepishly. It turned out she'd swiped the dress off my laundry pile and worn it to a lecture.

Being generous with your clothes can pay dividends. After the student house came a flatshare with two friends – and, crucially, their very nice clothes, where I borrowed as much as I bequeathed. It was like having two extra bonus wardrobes, both usually in better condition than mine. There was an embellished jumper I loved so much and wore so often that I 'accidentally' took it with me when I moved out.

In fact, I advocate a kind of squatters' rights for borrowed items. If they never wear the thing and you love it, after a certain amount of time has lapsed it becomes 'spiritually yours' and should pass over into your possession. Even now, my friend Sarah will regularly do a sweep of my bedroom asking 'when did you last wear this?', and if I can't put up a decent protest, into her bag it goes. That feels right, somehow. All the friends who have selflessly given up their time and energy to shopping trips and WhatsApp selfie parades deserve a payout. In my head the many, many clothes they've consulted on over the years belong a little, by extension, to them.

These days I don't have the housemates, but I still share clothes. I even have co-ownership of a coat with my friend Caroline, AKA @knickers_models_own, which we bought from my local charity shop on the day we met. It's a very good coat; a sturdy toffee-brown belted duster with strong vibes of Arkwright from Open All Hours. We both spotted it on a mannequin and pounced at the same time – but instead of an undignified tussle, she suggested we try a timeshare arrangement. Intrigued, I agreed.

Since then we've passed it back and forth between us every month or two, and through our handover meetings, which quickly became coffees and lunches, we've established a friendship. I like hearing about what the coat's been up to and seeing how she's styled it differently to me. Only having the coat on a part-time basis means that each time I get it back it feels fresh and exciting – like I've been shopping, but for free! – and we have passionate sartorial make-up sex. *Reunited, and it feels so good.*

If it spent the whole year in my cupboard, I'd probably wear it the same amount. Maybe less. The magic is in the illusion of newness, combined with the reliability of a coat I already know suits me.

Of course, this kind of organised polyamory isn't going to work for everyone. It requires willing participants who are roughly your size, and share your taste, and aren't going to get fussy about stretched sleeves or crumbs in pockets. But it works more often than you might think. At one time or another I've shared clothes with my friends, my brothers, my mother and my boyfriend (while my hips have laughed in the face of 'boyfriend' jeans since puberty, his uncommonly dainty feet mean I can nick his trainers).

And sure, there's the odd blip. There was a fantastic pair of white Mary Janes with four-inch block heels that I'd worn once – once! – before loaning them to a friend who never returned them. There was The Who T-shirt, which I bought on my first adolescent trip to Carnaby Street, lost for ever when a friendship ended before I could get it back. One friend shrunk a beloved red lurex minidress into a cropped top in the wash, which still makes me a little bit teary to think about.

As a lender you have every right to say no, or issue ground rules, especially if it's a family heirloom and there's a good reason people call your pal 'Calamity Jen'. But on balance the risk feels worth it, to spare the planet another needless purchase and fuel the circle of good clothes karma instead.

Besides the obvious financial and ethical benefits, there's something undeniably lovely about creating a piece of fashion history with another person. I feel a little swell of pride every time I get a text from a friend asking me to kit them out, or see one of my bits pop up on Instagram. My bag at a wedding; my tasselled kaftan on a far-flung sun lounger. It's nice to think those clothes are getting a bit more out of life than I alone could give them. One old dress, bought and loved when I was seventeen, was passed on to my friend Amy a few years ago and has now been claimed by her teenage niece, who is wearing it with considerable élan all round the Midlands. This makes me very happy.

So, either a borrower or a lender be! If you love something, you set it free. Whether it's peer-to-peer platforms, swishing parties, or just putting out the sartorial SOS on the group chat, the sustainable fashion of the future is open-source. Friends don't let friends waste money on another pastel wedding jacket. Caring is sharing.

Caring is also following the washing instructions, Flora. But it's okay, I'm over it now.

SELL, SELL, SELL

Good karma is priceless, but let's be honest – sometimes you just need the cash.

Thankfully it's never been so easy to make a quick buck from your cast-offs. The resale market is expected to double in the next five years, with some projections saying pre-owned sales could actually overtake fast fashion within a decade.[137] As part of the move towards a circular economy, selling our unloved stuff has never made so much sense.

For many years our main options were eBay or analogue, i.e. getting up at the crack of dawn to tout our wares at a car boot sale. But now, just like the rental market, there are new resale platforms popping up all the time. Most are pretty straightforward – you list it, you sell it, you post it – but each site or app has its own demographic and business model, so it pays to do your research and choose the right one.

Luxury resale is big, naturally. When you've dropped serious dollar on a designer label or 'investment' bag, the financial benefits are likely to outweigh the time commitment of photographing, measuring, describing, listing and posting – all of which can seem like a lot of effort for a Dorothy Perkins skater dress. Some swankier sites (like fash-pack favourite Vestiaire Collective) act as a concierge, vetting items for quality and authenticity before they're sent on to your buyer. Some are online consignment stores which charge commission on the final sale price (High Fashion Society charges 50 per cent, Hardly Ever Worn It a modest 18 per cent). And some, like Designer Exchange (which has real-life stores in London, Manchester, Birmingham and Leeds), will buy items directly from you before they sell them on and keep the profit.

But even your scrappier high-street buys can find a new home, through sites like Vinted (which charges no fee to list and sell items) or community-focused platforms like Shpock, Gumtree or Facebook Marketplace, which will save you a trip to the Post Office by finding a buyer just up the road.

I'm still misty-eyed about the pair of Miss Selfridge x Terry de Havilland platforms I bought for a fiver in the sale in 2005 and sold on eBay for £95, back when I was seventeen and £95 was riches beyond my wildest dreams. Alas, it wasn't the beginning of a glittering career as a Dotcom Del Boy, but despite now charging a 10 per cent seller's fee, eBay remains one of the best places to sell your stuff. Use an online fee calculator like finalfeecalc.co.uk to work out in advance how much you could make, and whether it's worth the hassle.

Then there's Depop, the young upstart on its way to becoming the grandaddy of them all. Like Instagram with added e-commerce, Depop's strength is in its social media DNA. You can curate your feed, follow, comment and direct-message sellers, and then you can click to buy. Photos are often styled with influencer-level sass, and sold items remain on a user's grid so we can see what we could have won.

The formula has proved irresistible, especially to teenagers with time on their hands. The app now has more than 13 million users, 90 per cent of whom are aged under twenty-six, and re-selling has become an established route for Gen Z-ers with entrepreneurial aspirations.[138] Everything from Balenciaga to Boohoo can be found on Depop, and it's a booming marketplace for young designers, upcyclers and streetwear traders, with some top sellers reportedly pocketing more than £150,000 a year.[139] Once you Depop, it's hard to stop.

The app's sheer abundance can be a downside too, as all except the most painfully specific of searches can throw up a lot of dross. When it comes to secondhand there's no way of sorting last century's styles from last season's (users will tag anything #vintage if it's been worn once for more than an hour), and the barrage of hashtag spam can make it hard to filter the genuine preloved items from sweatshop T-shirts and knock-off sneakers.

But like everything, we get out what we put in. To maximise your chances of an online sale, take the time to photograph your stuff from all angles, in natural light, and ideally on a human rather than drooping sadly off your wardrobe door. List the garment's measurements as well as the label size, especially for vintage pieces, and include as much relevant info (#80s #denim #bananarama #acidwash) as you can, but not irrelevant info (#Gucci #OslenTwins #CBD #Brexit). Always be honest about flaws. Many buyers won't mind about a small hole, but they'll be pissed off if it's a surprise.

And for all this to work, remember sustainable shopping needs to be a two-way street. We have to support the resale market by buying from it too, not just flog our old clothes to make room for new ones. Let's do our best to not see it as a way to beat the system (she says, wearing BNIB Vagabond boots from eBay), but more as an extension of the sharing economy, and all the goodwill that comes with it. It's the circle of clothes, and it moves us all.

VINTAGING GRACEFULLY

One of the most straightforward solutions for our fast-fashion problem is obvious: buy old clothes.

Some 64 per cent of people are now 'willing' to shop pre-owned, apparently, compared to 45 per cent just two years ago – and it's projected that by 2028 around 13 per cent of the clothes in our wardrobes will be secondhand.[141] Even that sounds low, when you consider how much barely rumpled 'used' clothing will be floating around by then, the leftovers of our fast-fashion appetites. All signs point to a future where we'll make secondhand our first port of call, and the high street a last resort. #Secondhandfirst, as the hashtag has it.

But secondhand is one thing; *vintage* is another, darling.

While the word is often bandied about to mean anything vaguely left of Cath Kidston, in technical terms 'vintage' usually refers to clothes that are at least twenty years old. Still though, that means anything dating back to the Millennium now qualifies. Your old Kickers are vintage. The handkerchief top I wore to my middle school leavers' disco is vintage. Robbie Williams' sex appeal is vintage. Let's ruminate on that for a minute.

Between the ages of about seventeen and twenty, back when the term meant strictly pre-Live Aid, I dressed pretty much entirely in vintage. I was one of those kids. Every school and college has a few; the nostalgia fetishists and bedroom poets, painfully self-conscious in most respects yet somehow unafraid of rocking up to lectures in an 80s ballgown and a beret. Andie from *Pretty in Pink* without the love interests, that was me.

I wore vintage clothes partly as a visual signifier that I was *cultured* and *eclectic* and yes I would *love* to come and see your band play, and partly because I felt starkly unwelcome on the high street, which in the mid-noughties was going through its skinny-jeans-Kate-Moss-for-Topshop-American-Apparel-hotpants phase and had no room, often literally, for me.

But still, I was proud (smug) of my original aesthetic (parade of ropey polyester). I was proud when local kids yelled, 'Oi, it's 2004 not 1964!' at me in the street, I was proud when my friend Lizzie's mum used to make me 'explain' my outfit to her on the doorstep, and I was even proud when dancing at sticky-floored club nights would cause a body odour to waft up from my dress that wasn't, I would realise a few seconds later, my own.

I was also greedy. Just as acquisitive as I have been with fast fashion, or more. I could afford to be, because this wasn't your premium £100-a-pop vintage; it was scrappy dresses plucked out of bargain bins in Rokit, shovelled into carrier bags at kilo sales or bought for £3.87 in late-night eBay sessions and forgotten about by the time they arrived in the post. Surprise! Another floral shirtwaister for your Princess Diana memorial collection!

By my second year of uni I had a hundred vintage dresses – all of them creased, many of them slashed into minis and badly hemmed at 2am with bright-green thread – and I was inordinately proud of that too. I was hungry for fashion history and wanted to *own it all*, to sweep decades' worth of style into my wardrobe by the armful. There were more discerning contestants on *Supermarket Sweep*.

I loved many of the dresses, but I messed around many more. I would wear them out once, feel frumpy, chop the hem off, feel worse, then relegate them to the back of the wardrobe. It was sustainable fashion, yes, but worn in the least conscious way. Not that 'mindful consumption' was much of a priority back then. If it had been, there'd have been fewer kebab stains on the dresses.

Anyway, to the anguish of my juvenile self, none of this makes me very original. Lots of us go through a vintage phase, much like we go through a purple hair phase or an occult phase. There's something about the teen psyche that produces these bursts of brilliant exhibitionism amid all the crippling self-consciousness. When you're young and awkward, unsure of yourself and painfully aware of the way everyone else sees you, there's a perverse pleasure to be found in dressing as anyone but yourself. 'Today I won't be Gemma, geography prefect – I shall be Gigi, Queen of the Steampunk Fairies!' The confidence flows hot and strong in front of the bedroom mirror in the morning, but often dries up by the time you're on the train wearing a top hat and a bustle, being side-eyed by half of Bognor Regis.

But once we grow up, our schedules fill up and our identities start to calcify, vintage shopping can feel like a whole other ball game. Where retro dressing once felt liberating, it can start to feel silly. Ostentatious. Try-hard.

Or maybe you hate the idea of it, and feel that vintage clothes = musty, moth-eaten throwbacks. Or maybe you like the idea of it, but not the time and energy needed to trawl through markets and vast warehouse shops, tentatively sniffing at armpits. Maybe your nearest vintage store is fifty miles away, and only opens every second Tuesday.

Maybe your reservations are one or more of the following. In which case, I have answers.

1. What you just said about sniffing armpits

I know, the smell. But it's fixable! Please proceed to page 234, where I promise things are meadow-fresh.

2. I can't pull it off

Part of the problem, I think, is that for a long time vintage has been seen as a bid to be cool or 'alternative', setting up camp on the other side of some imagined social fence that was first erected in high school. Even though fast fashion mines the history books constantly, serving infinite rehashes of old shapes, prints and styles, wearing authentically retro clothes still carries connotations of a certain lifestyle. A kind of studied, self-conscious whimsy. The suggestion you might spend your weekend doing the lindy hop at classic-car conventions.

'I think lots of people are worried about looking too "costume",' agrees Laura Von Behr, one of my favourite London vintage traders, who has a knack for styling her clients in a way that always feels bang up to date. The answer, unsurprisingly, is mixing things up. 'With separates it's easier, because you can have that element, a nod to something,' she says. 'But if you've got a really full-on dress, let's say a 60s pop-print dress . . .' Don't have a beehive? 'Exactly. Just do a more natural tousled look. Likewise shoes and earrings – don't have matching 60s accessories. You've just got to relax it.'

The same is true for fabric; relax it. The least successful vintage buys are usually the ones made from stiff, heavy material or with stiff, heavy linings. This is the 21st century; we prize fluidity. So swerve anything that you can't comfortably move and breathe in, no matter how beautiful the shape – especially if you're going to wear it in summer, or take it within ten feet of a dancefloor. You'll end up feeling stuffy and awkward in a puddle of sweat, and you won't wear it twice.

Vintage purists might say trends are the devil, but ignore them. In fact, if you're nervous, I recommend keeping one eye on the high street. Look at what's in the shops, look at what people are wearing in the street, and stay consistent with one or two details like collars, prints or hemlines. If everyone else is wearing long midis, knee-length vintage can feel oddly frumpy – but a maxi taken up a few inches could be perfect. If peasant blouses or leaf prints or button-down A-lines are everywhere, track down a vintage version. Instead of buying fashion's latest rehash, go and find the real McCoy.

None of these trends are new, remember. They were making them before we were born.

3. I can't pull it *on*

There are no two ways about it: vintage sizing sucks.

People will tell you it's because humans have got bigger. As time has moved on, diets have changed and we've been freed from the shackles of corsetry and ration books, so our bodies have changed too. Clothes have grown gradually larger to accommodate our evolving shapes, meaning vintage sizes are skewed on a curve (and less likely to do up over ours).

I like to call this 'The Monroe Conspiracy' after the popular fallacy beloved by aunties on Facebook the world over, that Marilyn Monroe was a size 16. She may well have been, but a 1950s size 16 is more like a modern day 10/12. One vintage trader told me that size 8 customers will often balk when a retro size 14 fits them like a glove. Naturally this makes those of us who wear a size 14 or larger feel fantastic.

But let's get this straight – plus-size women have always existed, much as fashion might have tried to pretend otherwise. They've always existed, just not always been accommodated. That's why the majority of plus-size clothes dating back pre-1980s tend to be homemade, because all the Bettys and Susans who weren't catered for by the shops were forced to take matters into their own hands.

There's a 'survival bias' in vintage that mirrors, frustratingly, mainstream fashion, with smaller sizes tending to be the ones that are preserved and passed on. 'A lot of vintage sellers will just buy things that are tiny, knowing that a lot of the time they'll sell it for design inspiration. So they're not bothered,' says Laura Von Behr. 'That does need to change. Maybe that's what's putting off a lot of people.' I'd say it's a safe bet.

The good news is that plenty of modern vintage sellers feel differently, Von Behr included, and put the effort into sourcing a wider range of sizes and in styles more exciting than a rack of kaftans. It's also worth remembering that good vintage, especially at the older end, will often have ample seam allowance in a way that modern fast fashion doesn't – those extra centimetres of fabric eat into profit margins, after all – so old clothes can often be taken out or lengthened to fit you perfectly.

The better news is that these days we have something Betty and Susan didn't: the internet. Trawling online is no substitute for the joy of a physical rummage in a vintage shop or market, but it is a great way to bypass the misery of an afternoon spent trying to zip up dresses seemingly designed before ribs had been invented.

Size-inclusive traders aren't always easy to find – Google 'plus-size vintage' and you're met with page after page of rockabilly petticoats (putting a woman in cat-eye glasses on the tag it doesn't make it 'vintage' any more than this bottle of £2.99 Aldi *vin de table* is 'vintage', lads) – but they are out there. VenusVintageClothing on Etsy stocks size 14–28, and US-based Champagne Lava exclusively stocks size L and above. Beyond Retro's online store has plus-size vintage sections for women and men. Depop boutique Salvaged Project makes a point of sourcing vintage pieces over a size 18. A search for size 18+ vintage on ASOS Marketplace just now returned an encouraging 309 results. It's not loads, but it's something.

Once you get into the groove, you'll find that certain styles and eras fit better than others. While I want to believe the 1960s were my spiritual decade, they were also a time when fashion fetishised narrow hips and flat chests, and as a result those modish silhouettes are the ones I most regularly find myself getting stuck in behind a rattan screen while a kindly assistant offers to oil the zip. Meanwhile the 50s and 70s were bigger fans of T&A (that's tits and ass, not tab and amphetamines), so those are the sections I gravitate towards. You might be the opposite, though, in which case please buy every funnel-necked shift dress on my behalf.

'I would say it's mostly about knowing what you're looking for and knowing your style. Knowing which designers make designs for your body,' agrees Aja Barber, who buys the majority of her clothes secondhand. 'It also helps to not be afraid to try things on. I've bought tops secondhand and added a panel of fabric so that it would fit me. I know *we shouldn't have to do this,* but I'm all about making it work.'

'We shouldn't have to do this but I'm all about making it work' is now this book's unofficial subtitle.

4. I will end up spending £300 out of politeness

I know the scenario you're dreading. You wander into a vintage shop, perhaps to kill a bit of time or have a casual rummage, and before you know it you're starring in a kind of hipster *Mr Benn*. As if by magic, the shopkeeper appears.

'Hiiii!' they beam, with the air of one who hasn't had human contact in several hours. You begin to sweat.

'Hiii!' you reply, mentally calculating the shortest route back to the door.

'Do you need any hel—'

'JUST HAVING A BROWSE,' you bleat, like a cornered lamb.

Now you must perform the role of Person Just Having a Browse, doing that special slow walk we also do in art galleries. You flip through the racks. You idly stroke a sleeve. 'OH THAT'S A LOVELY ONE,' they yell from across the room.

Mm, you murmur in agreement, because what else are you going to say?

'YOU CAN TRY IT ON IF YOU LIKE!'

Thanks, you say, but it doesn't look quite your size.

'You'd be surprised!' they continue, suddenly at your elbow. 'The only way to find out is to try it on!'

Really, it's fine, you insist – but before you know it, you have spent half a month's rent on a cowl-necked jumpsuit with accompanying cape under the promise it makes you look like a young Donna Summer. Or did they say Donald Sumpter? Anyway, too late.

The other week I encountered a vintage trader who ordered me to come out of the fitting room to show her each item I tried on, *even if it didn't fit*, so she could manhandle the zip and say helpful things like 'just another three inches and it'd be perfect!'. To be clear, you are not obliged to do this. It's not part of the authentic vintage experience. Nor do you have to put up with the opposite: being patronised and sneered at by someone with an ironic mullet.

But, once you relax into it, the personal service is one of the genuine perks of secondhand shopping. I promise. Good vintage traders are an invaluable untapped source of styling advice, specialist knowledge and infectious enthusiasm. Make friends with your local one and it pays dividends: they will look out for things to suit you, give you dibs on new stock, hook you up with tailors and cobblers, and tell you stories of all the former lives your purchase might have had.

The best shopkeepers act as a conduit to help you form that all-important emotional attachment to your clothes.

They make shopping an occasion again, rather than just an anonymous transaction.

Or if worst comes to it, you can just pretend you don't speak English.

5. It's all too much effort

It is effort, I won't lie. Vintage shopping can be a time-drain, a physical strain and occasionally an allergen nightmare. But then so can going to three branches of H&M in an hour.

Besides, it's worth it when you find *that* piece, the show-stopping thing that makes your heart beat a little faster and Rod Stewart singing 'You Wear It Well' magically strike up on the stereo. *A little old-fashioned, but that's alright.* The thing that fits so well it's borderline creepy, as though you might be taking part in one of those dual-timeline novels with a version of yourself from 1976. It's worth it when someone asks where your clothes are from and you get to answer, radiating smugness, 'Oh, this? It's vintage.'

Take it from a reformed vintageaholic: while it's easy to get caught up in the illusion of 'guilt-free' shopping and buy any old thing that crosses your path, the good stuff lasts and lasts. In fact, vintage finds will reinvent themselves to suit the person you are at many junctures in your life. They'll greet you like an old friend every time you pull them out of the wardrobe. If fast fashion sells us all the same story, vintage helps us write an epic saga.

There was a striped trapeze-line mini with polka dot sleeves that came to define my fresher's experience. I'm wearing it in so many photos you could be forgiven for thinking I only went to one party all year (when in fact it was at least three!). I still have that dress now, cuffs a little frayed, and I still take it out every so often to hold it up in front of the mirror, and descend into one of those nostalgia trips that begins with an anecdote about 80p vodbulls and ends three hours later, knee deep in The Cribs' back catalogue.

It's easy to get quasi-spiritual about vintage clothes; the memories upon memories, the legacies of previous owners layered up with your own, all mingling with the ghostly trace of some long-ago perfume. But if that's not your bag, *that's okay too*.

These days vintage shops vary almost as much as 'normal' shops do, driven by different demographics and passions, from pristine high-end boutiques and antique showrooms to giant bargain basements. With nearly a hundred years of archives to choose from, there is no one vintage 'look' anymore than there is one 20th-century 'look' – it's an umbrella that encompasses 90s streetwear and pre-war tea dresses; the grungy, the groovy and the thoroughly prim.

In fact, and I am sorry for anyone to whom this might be news, 'Y2K' is now a legit style category. They're clamouring for Juicy Couture velour all over Depop as we speak. And as fast fashion's relentless pace has us sampling increasingly recent eras (what's that coming over the hill, is it the Punkyfish renaissance?), it feels like we're approaching a point where the distinction between 'vintage' and 'secondhand' starts to disappear altogether.

1966 or 2016? Ultimately, who cares, if you love it and you're keeping it out of landfill.

The vintage world has its elitists and purists just like anything else, and yet as time goes on and our collective wardrobe crisis grows more urgent, it feels like we should put aside those snobberies for the greater good of getting more people into old clothes. One day, hopefully before the clothes hanging in Zara right *now* qualify as vintage, they'll be the 'normal' shops.

The six commandments of vintage shopping

1. I will take my time

Nipping-in is for advanced-level thrifters only, so block out a leisurely afternoon and let yourself enjoy the rummage. It's all part of the process.

2. I will always do a second lap

Somehow you never notice the best stuff on the first round, so always comb every rack in the shop at least twice. Think of it like double-cleansing.

3. I will ignore the size on the label

Always go by measurements, if you can find any. If not, there's the neck test. Your neck is roughly half the circumference of your waist – so if a waistband fits comfortably round your neck when folded in half, then it should fit your waist too. Sounds implausible, but it's true. This is how I discovered I'd look great in an Elizabethan ruff.

4. I will be eagle-eyed

Check everything carefully for holes, stains and missing buttons before you buy. You could still buy it anyway, as a repair job, but at least you can haggle a bit off the price for any flaws not marked 'as seen'.

5. I will not expect success every time

The hit rate is lower for secondhand shopping, but that's kind of the point. 'Always be prepared to leave empty-handed,' agrees Caroline Jones. 'Creating a beautiful, hard-working wardrobe that gives you multiple styling options *should* take time.' So if you don't find your soulmate on this trip, do not be cajoled into buying something you don't love just because it's cheaper than new. Take inspiration instead. Take notes, even. Write down the labels you like, and check eBay and Etsy for something similar when you get home. Or just try again another day. Vintage isn't going anywhere.

6. I will not shop while pre-menstrual

Unless it's for soft cookies. That's just common sense.

A few words on smells

One of the most common issues people tend to have with secondhand clothes – and especially in the vintage world, where having several decades of olfactory history baked into the armpits is sometimes waved off as part of the charm – is their smell. This is entirely fair. I'm not about to tell you that you should be wearing a retro stranger's bodily musk as an eco-warrior badge of honour.

The good news is that these days charity shops and vintage stores tend to steam everything before it hits the shop floor, meaning they're arguably fresher and more sterile than your average high-street shipment. I'll wear things straight off the rails without so much as a Febreze first, and I promise nobody is backing away in horror or breathing through their scarf next to me on the train. That I've noticed.

But that doesn't mean the odd BO infusion doesn't slip through the net, nor the occasional item steeped in half a century's worth of dust. The worst culprits tend to be the junkier experiences – markets, jumble sales, antique shops, those surprise vintage stalls you come across in weird places like church fetes and garden centres. They tend to be the cheapest too. The bigger the bargain, the more likely you are to have to deal with some laundry admin.

But the good news is, with a little elbow grease, nearly every smell is reversible. Even elbow grease. 'You have to remember that it's usually a collective smell, when you walk into those thrift shops. And as long as you give it a good airing, you can generally shift it,' promises Laura Von Behr.

Don't just fling it in the wash and hope for the best. Take a more targeted approach, particularly with older pieces that might fall apart in the machine. Locate the smell. Treat the smell. Repeat if necessary. Imagine the garment is an old stray dog and you are the benevolent vet nursing it lovingly back to health.

In fittingly old-fashioned style, Laura says the best cure of all is fresh air. 'Basically I think there's nothing better than hanging it in a gale for as long as possible,' she says, and she's right. But for those of us without gardens, there are indoor options too.

Bicarbonate of soda is a good hack, because its mild alkaline quality neutralises the acidic compounds that make up most bodily pongs. Either add half a cup to a sinkful of cold water and soak your clothes for several hours (don't risk soaking anything very old, in case it falls apart), or make a paste of bicarb and water and apply it straight to the offending region. For shoes that stink, add a generous sprinkle of dry bicarbonate of soda (please note: not baking powder) and leave them overnight, then shake out in the morning.

Confusingly, vinegar is a wardrobe hero for the opposite reason. Its acetic acid content helps to blast out smells, and provided you follow up with some gentle handwash liquid and rinse well, it shouldn't replace them with *eau de chip shop*. Add a cup of distilled white vinegar (please note: not balsamic) to a sinkful of cold water and soak the item, inside-out, for several hours or overnight.

There's also activated charcoal – just pop a couple of briquettes in a sealable bag with the garment and leave it for up to a week – and you can even try spritzing with diluted vodka, which will give you an air of louche debauchery if nothing else. Or as a last resort, try putting it in the freezer for a few days. Keep it separate from the Magnums. Do not defrost in the microwave.

All of this might sound like a lot of effort, but a few domestic adventures are worth it to shift the danced-all-night-smoking-Player's-No.6-while-sweating-out-a-steak-Diane whiff you somehow failed to notice in the shop. After all, there's nothing I find improves an outfit like being able to lift your arms up while wearing it.

Besides, have you smelled fast fashion recently? That weirdly vinegary 'new clothes' smell, the scent of distant warehouses and packing crates, sawdust and chemicals? It's hardly a bouquet of roses either. Fetid pits might not be anyone's dream accessory, but at least they suggest someone had fun in your clothes first.

'The charity that is a trifle to us can be precious to others.'

– Homer, *The Odyssey*[142]

SWEET CHARITY

I love charity shops. I was raised on them, and in them. My parents love charity shops so much they plan holidays around them (did you know, Bexhill-on-Sea has sixteen within a few streets?), and my childhood memories are peppered with afternoons rifling through strange bric-a-brac, yellowing paperbacks and racks of St Michael blouses in search of buried treasure.

We shopped in them out of necessity, when money was tight and my brothers and I insisted, stubbornly, on growing. But also out of curiosity and a certain romanticism for the past, and because wandering round the corner to the Scope shop was less stressful than schlepping us all into town. While they didn't have the high glamour of Tammy Girl or New Look 915, to my young self charity shops represented freedom, possibility, or at least better odds. If you wanted something from Oxfam, the grown-ups were much more likely to say yes.

Only when I got older did I realise this wasn't the way everyone's parents felt about charity shops. The stigma lingers on, although it's fading. Dead people's clothes.

Poor-people clothes. Dust, decay, old tissues in the pockets. In a culture fixated on the shiny and new, it's hardly a surprise that for many people charity shops are still seen as a source of shame. But that itself is a shame, because their power extends well past saving money.

The overachievers of the sustainable fashion world, charity shops do good in quadruplicate. They save clothes from landfill (327,000 tonnes of textiles in 2018 alone), and stop us buying new ones.[143] They raise vital funds for important causes. They provide access to low-cost clothing for the many people who need it, and they offer valuable skills-training, support and company for volunteers from all walks of life. Including freelancers who need to escape their laptop for a few hours and remember how to converse with humans (hi). A charity shop is a port in the storm, a pillar of the community, and a place to shelter from the rain when your bus isn't due for eight minutes. They're a place to go when you have nowhere to go, and for that alone they deserve protecting.

But they're also a place to go when you have nothing to wear. Trust me on this.

Donations are at an all-time high, and charities are working harder than ever to present themselves as a credible fashion alternative. 'Charity shops are bucking the trend in UK high-street retail and recorded four consecutive quarters of growth in 2018,' confirms Mark Chapman from the Charity Retail Association. 'As more people become aware of sustainable fashion and environmental issues, I'm sure this can only lead to charity shops being seen as an ever-increasing "safe bet".'

He's right; we're moving closer to being able to use charity shops like 'normal' shops. Not just for kooky one-offs or Halloween hauls, but as reliable places to meet all your shopping briefs. Everyday basics, workwear, holiday wear, maternity wear, sportswear, partywear – and sometimes only a few steps behind the high street. Want a trench coat? A barely scuffed pair of Converse? Another Breton? Hit up enough charity shops and you'll find them sooner or later.

The perverse truth is that as fashion has got faster, charity shops have got better. While clothes move through our lives at breakneck speed, their stock gets refreshed faster too – so fast it can trigger a kind of sartorial deja vu. Oh look, a dress you tried on in the store six months ago! Already swallowed by someone else's wardrobe and spat back out again! It's exciting and depressing how frequently you can find clothes with the tags still attached – both a symptom of the problem, and its cure. But hey, it's great news for the squeamish. All the ethical benefits of secondhand trousers with only the *merest* memory of someone else's crotch.

And it's not all last season's Atmosphere, or those pleather coin belts from 2002. Everyone's heard the story of the friend of a friend of a friend who unearthed a Chanel 2.55 for £2.55 or whatever, but designer loot is more than just urban legend. Over the years I've personally seen, with my own eyes, Chloé, Marni, Gucci, Louis Vuitton, Ralph Lauren, Marc Jacobs, Céline, McQueen and Dior all cosying up on charity shop rails. In fairness they were all priced by people who knew their labels, or at least had access to Google – but then you can hardly begrudge a charity trying to make the most bang for its buck. They're moral multi-taskers, remember.

Ever since retail guru Mary Portas launched her first branch of Mary's Living & Giving with Save the Children in 2009, there has been a noticeable rise in 'boutique' chazzers: airy, spacious and stocked with a more curated, premium selection than usual. They're a bold attempt to attract a more fashion-forward demographic, not just for the prof-its but for the whole sector's image. When Shelter opened its unashamedly hip Boutique at Coal Drops Yard, a new £100m shopping and dining complex in London's King's Cross designed by architect Thomas Heatherwick, it planted a new flag for charity shops. Once they were viewed by councils and developers as a marker of deprivation; now they're finally being championed as part of a sustainable future.

While thrift shoppers might still feel like a niche gang, we're actually a global majority – 70 per cent of the world's population uses mainly secondhand clothing, although dis-proportionate amounts of those clothes were once ours.[144] The UK is the second biggest exporter of used clothing in the world, after the US. Our charity shops often get more donations than they can physically handle, without enough demand to shift them all on the shop floor. And so they're sold on, most often to sub-Saharan Africa, where imports of used clothes are reaching record levels. WRAP estimates that around two-thirds of donated clothes now end up overseas. We're casting them off, twice over.

As journalist Sophie Benson reported for *Grazia* last year, exporting our old clothes still raises funds for the charities, but it comes at a price for the countries receiving them. 'The never-ending wave of second-hand clothing that floods the shores of Africa sells for as little as 5 or 10 per cent of the cost of a new, locally made garment, undercutting domestic textile industries,' she writes. 'Not only does this put skilled makers and merchants out of work, but it makes African nations dependent on our donations, stifling home-grown development.'[145] Obviously, this doesn't mean we should stop donating to charity shops. But rather than using them like friendly recycling bins, we need to support them with our custom too.

So what's stopping us? Most charity shops take card payments these days, so your lack of luddite cash is no excuse. They have decent changing rooms and recycled carrier bags. Many accept returns. The shop I volunteer at stays open till 7pm on weeknights to accommodate the commuter crowd. You can buy charity loot online too; the Oxfam site has one of the best secondhand selections on the whole internet, each item lovingly described with measurements, details on fit and fabric, and styling suggestions. Thrift+ will send you a cardboard box to fill up with donations for the charity of your choice, sell them online and give you 33 per cent back in credit. You can even buy Oxfam, TRAID and Barnardo's on ASOS now, for god's sake. Dead people's clothes have never looked so healthy.

But while the high-end boutiques and the hi-spec tech are both welcome developments, we still need all kinds of charity shops to reflect the kinds of shoppers and dressers we are. Personally I'd be very sad to lose the trad ones, the musty jumble-sale kind that smell of three-bar heaters, with carousels of crinkly Mills & Boons and a pensioner behind the counter labelling everything 50p. And I don't think we will for a while. The average charity shop transaction is still just £3.89, so don't listen to anyone who says they're all extortionate these days. Or tell them to get out of Clapham.

Emma Slade Edmonson is something of a rock star in the world of secondhand shopping. A stylist, strategic consultant and creative director, she founded Charity Fashion Live, which re-created looks from the London Fashion Week catwalks in real time using charity-shop finds, and works on store revamps and campaigns to help lure a younger, digitally dependent crowd out to charity shops. In our flat-screen world, charity shops, she says, are 'about as authentic, connected a shopping experience as you can get'.

But it helps to have tactics. Emma recommends approaching with a certain occasion or item in mind ('if you're unprepared, charity shopping can feel a little like shopping on Boxing Day'), taking along a key piece from your wardrobe to build new outfits around, and looking out for something she calls 'the golden rail'. We know how I feel about rails.

'Now I can't promise it will always be there, but in my experience there will often be a special rail somewhere on the floor with many of the best goodies on it. In some shops this will be a vintage rail and in others it may have some recent Stella McCartney on it, for example. Have a look for it on your first few visits and soon you'll develop a knack for spotting it within minutes of entering the shop.'

And of course, the no.1 rule of charity shopping is: know your postcode. Posh neighbourhoods are typically the best for finding designer labels and heirlooms, everyone knows that. But it doesn't necessarily mean they're the most fashion-forward. If Aquascutum macs and yachting shoes don't float your boat, try places with a high proportion of elderly residents (great vintage and knitwear, excellent crockery), students (all those regrettable loan day hauls) or bougie thirty-somethings (Toast and Cos coming out of their ears). And to maximise your returns, do a crawl. My favourite thrifting destination is Edinburgh, where Morningside, Stockbridge and Portobello each have enough charity shops to occupy a whole afternoon. Pack snacks, you'll need your strength.

TRAID CEO Maria Chenoweth tells me that their shop locations are all part of the charity's strategy. Found in bustling but not salubrious neighbourhoods, TRAID stores are keen to differentiate themselves from the 'boutiques'. 'I want to be like the supermarket, where everyone can find something,' she says. 'I want to serve a really big, diverse community, not just a select few.'

TRAID is famous in London for its £1 sales, which result in 'a big orgy of people rampaging round the shop', and Chenoweth sees no reason they shouldn't still embrace the call to haul. 'Yes, I'm encouraging consumption,' she shrugs, 'but that is a displacement effect, I hope. Everyone who came and shopped with us shopped here, instead of going down the high street.' Charity shops are for realists, after all. When that urge to shop becomes overwhelming, they're the best place to scratch the itch.

And in case anyone is still under the impression that second-hand means second rate, Chenoweth is a model ambassador for chaz shop chic. 'I think I look fabulous and smart today,' she preens, talking me through her outfit: a white 80s blouse, cashmere cardigan, brown button-down pencil skirt ('it's got a stain on it') and leather and suede ankle boots ('they've given me bunions'). Thrifters love doing this, I've noticed; pointing out the flaws even as we're showing off our prize finds. To the uninitiated it might sound like insecurity, but it's actually more like defiance. A way to flick a finger at fast fashion's cult of pristine newness. Look, we say, I'm holey and I'm stained and I'm *fierce*.

Whether it's clothes swapping, jostling over the best Jaeger at the WI sale or a blaze of fire emojis under our Instagram posts, sustainable dressing should be about community and camaraderie, and charity shops perhaps most of all. Sure, there are moments when you're tempted to keep your sources secret (we've all recommended a great shop with our mouths while screaming 'BACK OFF MY SIZE 7s, BITCH!' with our brains) but ultimately, it's hard to be a secondhand shopper without believing in karmic retribution. We pay it forward. The universe gifts us a gem; we thank it by helping someone else find one too.

During all the years I was hitting up fast fashion at my hardest, charity shops remained a place of comfort and solace. And as the revolving door of ASOS, Topshop, Zara et al entered my wardrobe and left again looking worse for wear, it was the charity-shop finds I hung on to longer. Even though sometimes they were from ASOS, Topshop, Zara et al to begin with. Which is another funny thing about secondhand shopping – often you'll be drawn to stuff you'd never look twice at on the high street. In a different context, without the intoxicating fumes of rampant capitalism addling your brain, it's easier to know if you really like something or if you're just being swayed by the pressure to shop, shop, shop.

The frustration of a secondhand garment, of course, is that there's only one of it. No asking for another size, or another colour, or one without a giant hole in the crotch. But after the relentless treadmill of fast fashion, with its 'infinite monkey theorem' promise that if you just try enough shops and websites for a long enough time eventually one will produce the ultimate outfit, that simplicity can also be a blessed relief. In a charity shop, destiny is your stylist and fate your personal shopper. Either it fits, or it doesn't. Either it's meant to be yours, or it isn't.

Sometimes it's coincidence enough to make you shiver, as though the universe has placed something there especially for you – like the time I walked into the charity shop at the end of my road and found boxfresh pink Adidas Gazelles in my size for £8, having almost bought the exact same pair for £80 the week before. I *know*.

You don't even really 'shop' in charity shops. There's a whole other set of verbs, more charming ones. You potter. You rummage. You pootle round. The activity itself is enough, without necessarily buying anything. We're hobbyists, us charity shop nerds, high on the whiff of possibility and glowing with moral kudos. If we were dealing in guilt, which of course we're not, I'd say it's the closest we can get to 'guilt-free' shopping. Even better, it's active, productive shopping, to know that each new-old handbag or broken-in pair of jeans takes us slightly closer to curing cancer, or ending homelessness, or de-worming a cat.

So even if they're never going to be the backbone of your future wardrobe, do me a favour and pay them a visit. Support your local charity shop. Take your bag of cast-offs, then stay for a forage. A plunder. A snoop. Today might be the day you get lucky.

I told you they take contactless, didn't I?

Agents of change

The main problem with dress agencies is the fact they're called 'dress agencies', which inevitably makes them sound like places to buy a debutante gown or a Mother of the Bride frock coat. And sometimes they are. But more often, they're shops full of clean, pristine and highly desirable clothes that perfectly bridge the gap between fast and slow fashion. Secondhand shopping for people who are scared of secondhand shopping, if you will.

Dress agencies, called 'consignment stores' in the US, work like this: customers bring in unwanted clothes, shoes and accessories (usually only a few seasons old, but sometimes high-quality vintage) and the shop sells them in exchange for 50 per cent of the profit. Stock is seasonal and only stays on the floor for a few weeks, to keep things fresh. Prices are often reduced after a certain amount of time on sale, and anything that doesn't get snapped up is returned to its owner or donated to charity. They're a good way to sell on the cream of your wardrobe if resale apps sound too much like hard work, but they're an even better way to shop the high street at one-removed.

As independent businesses, each store has its own approach, but the usual rule of 'posh area = spenny labels' stands. It's not all designer though; my local dress agency reliably has great items from Whistles, French Connection, Karen Millen, Cos, Topshop and the like for a third of the retail price, many of which are end-of-line deadstock and so completely unworn. I've bought sample Warehouse ankle boots there for £18, and a treasured Mother of Pearl silk skirt for £65. Which is a sustainable brand to begin with, so that's double the brownie points. Well done me.

If you're currently thinking 'dressy whatnows?', I guarantee there will be one in a nearby shopping precinct that you've probably walked past and ignored. Hit up dressagencydirectory.co.uk, which has more than five hundred fashion resale stores listed across the UK, to find your local.

'Fashion lives to express, delight, reflect, protest, comfort, commiserate and share. Fashion never subjugates, denigrates, degrades, marginalises or compromises. Fashion celebrates life.'

– Fashion Revolution[146]

ETHICALLY EVER AFTER

'But,' you might say, if you're the kind of clever dick I always end up talking to at barbecues, 'isn't "sustainable fashion" an oxymoron? Isn't fashion by its very definition *unsustainable*?'

It's a fair point. After all, the whole industry is built on keeping us in perpetual motion; an endless cycle of desire, acquisition and boredom. Is fashion that doesn't compel us to keep shopping still fashion? Or is it just ... *clothes*? I don't know. I do know I still can't see headlines like 'This 90s Pants Trend Is Back' without clicking through to find out which 90s pants trend is back. It may well be liberating to embrace a less conformist way of dressing, but I still want to know what I am or aren't conforming to.

'More and more, I find myself using the term "sustainable style" rather than "sustainable fashion",' says Clothes & The Rest's Holly Bullock. 'To me, "style" is more personal, more perennial and allows us to disconnect from the business of fashion, whilst still being engaged and excited by the clothes we wear.'

The battle of fashion vs style is nothing new; virtually every big designer, editor and fashion personality of the past hundred years has issued some glurge along the lines of 'Don't follow trends! True style is about being yourself!' It's sound advice, but it's also part of that retail negging we talked about. 'Don't follow fashion', they say, from inside the million pound house that fashion built. 'How vulgar!' they laugh, from their Porsche.

Truth is, fashion will always be part of our social fabric. It's human instinct to seek that buzz, of catching on to something at the same time someone else does – *oh my god, ME TOO* – and feeling part of a creative force bigger than yourself. 'Trends will have a place in sustainable fashion by default as they're a natural part of the ebb and flow of culture,' agrees Sophie Benson. 'But Western culture needs to adjust to celebrate individuality more so that we're not bound by trends, rather inspired to work them our own way, whether that's by customising what we already have or reaching back into the archives.'

That's the beautiful thing about post-millennial life, after all – we have a huge archive, ripe for the pillage. Ours is a generation of magpies, picking at a vast buffet of references rather than subscribing to a set menu. A 30s shape with a 70s print with an 80s jacket with a pair of 90s sneakers. Normcore one day, milkmaid the next. And while we might never live through anything that looks as outwardly anarchic as bondage trousers did the first time round, quiet revolutions are happening across the industry. We can still dress in protest and dissent; only this time it's swimsuits made from recycled fishing nets, and organic cotton slogan tees made by women paid a living wage. Our clothes can still kick against society, but only if we stop buying as many. Wearing the same outfit to three consecutive weddings feels like a more radical statement now than a mohawk and biker boots.

And, of course, sustainability is a hot trend itself. 'The buzzword of the season,' as I saw a fashion brand's blog call it the other day, apparently without irony.

The tide is turning; trickling in through in corners of the fashion media and awash in our social feeds. You can barely open a magazine or scroll Instagram without reading someone's declaration that they, too, are quitting fast fashion and pledging to buy less, buy better and tell us all about it. And it's great! I mean, it's terrible for me, a person trying to write a book about quitting fast fashion, buying less, buying better and telling you all about it – but it's great for the public consciousness. This is how fashion works, after all. The big idea, blooming large and unattainable at first and then drip, drip, dripping down to reach everyone.

It would be easy to rest on our laurels and assume that so much public noise means everything behind the scenes is heading in the right direction. But the reality is, about 40 per cent of the industry hasn't even moved beyond the initial stages of committing to improvement – just committing to it, let alone actually doing anything – and recent research suggests that sustainability progress might actually be slowing.[147] We are not finished. We are so far from finished.

What we need to do instead is something not even skinny jeans managed. We need to turn a trend into something permanent. We need to keep banging the drum, and resist the inevitable backslide. We need to keep wearing our clothes for longer, swapping them, sharing them, maintaining them, loving them, and all the while make it clear to the companies who would like to keep us on that trend treadmill: fashion is what we make it. Not what they tell us it is.

If Charlotte from *Sex and the City* is to be believed, it takes approximately half the time you were with someone to get over them after a break-up, which means the urge to run out and throw your pay cheque at the high street might take a few years yet to leave your system. Mine too.

The day I agreed to write this book, I was a few months into my shopping ban. I left the breakfast meeting with my publisher in a state of fizzing agitation, full of feelings – excitement, stress, fear, inspiration, but mainly an overwhelming urge to shop. Huh, I thought, as my legs gathered pace in the direction of Topshop. So that's still happening.

I steered myself away from Oxford Street, scene of so many crimes, and safely into vintage shop Beyond Retro. There I gathered up armfuls of clothes in a frenzy. I tried them all on, dithered, debated, and settled on a floral button-down dress and a midi skirt in monochrome jersey. Did I love them? Would I wear them thirty times? Yes! No. Maybe?

Who knew? I paid for them, dopamine-drunk, enjoying that familiar headrush as I punched my pin in and crumpled the receipt into my wallet. Then I went and had a panic attack in the toilets at Pret.

I wish I could tell you that those clothes, bought in the middle of whatever the hell emotional reaction I was having that morning, became symbols of my departure from fast fashion. A sartorial post-break-up haircut. I'd like to say I have worn them endlessly, loved them devotedly, cared for them like prize fiddle-leaf figs in the verdant utopia of my wardrobe. It would be such a neat ending.

But I can't, because if there's one thing I've learned on this journey, it's that nothing much can be tied up neatly. Nothing in life, but certainly not in the fashion industry, where the unruly mess of supply chains and stakeholder culpability could take decades to unravel and even longer to weave into something strong enough to sustain us all.

Last week, a man in my office asked me what I was working on. I told him – this book – and he sighed. 'But don't you think that we need a massive societal shift to ever solve the problems of fast fashion?'

Yes, I replied. I do. But what *is* a massive societal shift, if not the cumulative effect of millions of people all changing their habits in some minor, manageable way? After all, in the immortal words of the anthropologist Margaret Mead: 'Never doubt that a small group of thoughtful, committed citizens can change the world; indeed, it's the only thing that ever has.'

Or that's what I said in my head, when I thought of it an hour later. In reality I made a noise like 'mmhmhurr' and busied myself with the coffee machine.

You encounter a lot of whataboutery when you tell people you've quit fast fashion. Plenty of 'yes buts' and 'well actuallys' and people who want to tell you you're not doing enough, while simultaneously making you want to give up and do nothing at all.

At first, I thought I was confused because I didn't know enough. Now, having read a lot and spoken to people who know plenty, I realise that confusion is an inevitable part of all this. We're all confused, because it's confusing.

We tend to want a nice hierarchy, don't we? A clear set of rules. Good, better, best: tell me how to dress. But the reality is muddier than that and it's shifting all the time, as the world shifts and our priorities do too. The solution is never going to be as simple as 'secondhand trumps sustainable' or 'organic cotton wins!'. Everyone will have their own priorities and their own limitations, and we can't wait to stop being confused to start making a change.

Like being a vegetarian who sometimes has a drunken McNugget, imperfect efforts are so much more valuable than cynicism from the sidelines. I'll say it once more, for luck. We can only do the best we can do. *But most of us can probably do better than we are.*

We also can't create a truly sustainable future without acknowledging something we all wear – some of us lightly, some heavy as a velvet cloak. Privilege. Let's never forget that all this is a privilege. To have the education and resources to research supply chains is a privilege. So is being able to afford sustainable brands. So is having the time and ability to trawl charity shops, or to walk into a vintage shop knowing there will be options to fit you. It is a privilege to be able to flip open a fashion magazine and feel inspired and represented, rather than alienated and ignored. Having a platform as giant and luxurious as a whole book (a *book*!) in which to chew over my own half-formed ideas about all this is a giant privilege, and I only hope I've used it in a way that hasn't made you want to bite your own fist off.

But the wonderful thing is that we can all do our bit, even by doing nothing at all except getting dressed in the morning. Re-wearing our clothes should not be a radical act, and yet right now it feels like one. Let's step back and think for a second about how ludicrous that is. Really breathe it in. Dragging each item out of the trunk or wardrobe each summer should be accompanied by joy, not disappointment. 'It's that orange jumper again!' should be words that feel like praise, not judgement. This attitude shift isn't going to happen overnight, or even over a year, but we need to keep on going, wearing our clothes like heroes, again and again and again until we get there.

Of the two things I bought in Beyond Retro that day, I have worn the dress loads. I love it, it fits beautifully and once I'd snipped out the *Working Girl* shoulder pads, looks current but different enough to keep wearing long after the window displays have changed. With that dress, I aimed slightly north of the bullseye and hit the triple twenty.

The skirt, I do not love. Out of thirty wears, I have twenty-eight and a half left to go. The fit is weird, the length not quite right. The three tops I thought it would look so good with (yes, Mum) turned out to look . . . okay at best. I might swap it, or sell it, or donate it. I might find myself suddenly inspired to turn it into a cushion cover. Next time I might take a deep breath and ask myself a few more questions. It's pretty, it looks nice – *I don't have to have it.*

Unpicking those thought patterns takes time. I still look at other women in the street sometimes, become overwhelmed with envy at their clothes/shoes/bag and feel that urge to shop myself better. But what I've realised is: it never worked. Buying stuff never abated those feelings. If anything I felt *more* inadequate and envious back then, not less.

How will shopping look in the future? Fast fashion as we know it can't keep going at its current pace, so the high street as we know it has to change – probably beyond all recognition. But that doesn't mean our grandkids will never shop as a verb on a Saturday afternoon. It doesn't mean clothes as a cultural expression will slip off the agenda altogether, and cease to be a physical presence in our communities. At least, I hope not.

Rather than the gap-toothed high streets full of empty shops that we've grown used to seeing since the recession, slow-fashion campaigners want to see them become hives of local industry. Designer Rachel Clowes' vision is downright dreamy; a kind of Good Place neighbourhood for fashion lovers. She imagines: 'A mix of places to buy sustainable fashion, locally made fashion, tailors, repair shops, charity, secondhand and vintage shops, swap shops, rental/hire places. Places where you can learn to sew, knit, repair and alter. Workshops where you can see fashion designers, textile designers, makers, seamstresses, embroiderers and printers.' It's what Mary Portas calls 'social capital' – 'If you make places where people want to be, socially, then the economic capital follows.'[148]

Charity shop blogger Hannah Elliman wants to see respect for every stage of the supply chain mirrored on our labels. 'It would be great if there was a barcode on every item that you could scan and find out where the fabric came from, who dyed the fabric, who stitched the garment together, how it was transported to the shop, how far the garment has travelled in the whole process of being made, the environmental impact of the production of the garment and to be assured that everyone in this supply chain was paid fairly,' she says.

It's not an unrealistic dream. In April 2019, H&M announced that it was doing just this – customers can now scan a tag in-store and see a garment's whole production history.[149] Like Shazam, but for ethics! As long as we keep asking questions too, keep holding brands accountable and don't take these kinds of gestures as blanket assurance that they're doing everything right behind the scenes, we might get somewhere.

Personally, I want a future where buying secondhand clothes is more like buying a secondhand book or a refurbished laptop. On Amazon, we have the option to purchase a used book alongside a new one. Wouldn't it make sense to be able to walk into every Topshop, Warehouse and Zara in the kingdom and head straight for a 'preowned' section, or have our garments fixed in-store while we wait? The green shoots are sprouting – Patagonia runs a WornWear service re-selling used stock, and TOAST has been hosting Japanese sashiko repair sessions in stores for customers to have old items mended and transformed.

And while we're compiling a wishlist for Sustainability Santa Claus, I'd like a world where fashion magazines include secondhand clothes. Not because we could all go and elbow each other to the death for the same vintage skirt, but because that way mags could return to the purpose of inspiring us and informing us, rather than cajoling us into a lifestyle we can't sustain.

I know it's complicated. I know ad revenue from brands is often the only thing keeping these mags afloat. But I also know that nothing undermines your relatable, smart, 'everywoman' content like putting a £400 jumper on the next page. *Cosmopolitan UK* had Stacey Dooley on the cover of its May 2019 issue wearing top-to-toe Oxfam, which felt like a giant leap. One day, I hope it'll feel unremarkable.

But perhaps the longest overdue change we need to see is in representation. 'I'm excited about the direction the conversation is going with leadership,' says Aja Barber. 'I'm excited for a future where all of us feel we have a seat at the table and more of the leaders of the sustainable movement look like me.' The most sustainable clothes are the ones already in our wardrobe, but the most sustainable fashion industry is the one that throws open its doors wide and makes everyone feel welcome.

Breaking up with fast fashion will probably start out as an individual choice, something you want to do for yourself and maybe by yourself. For a while you might step back, opt out, decline the shopping invites, hide from the social ads. You might prefer not to broadcast it or brag about it while you give it a tentative go, and that's fine. We can't all write the book (please don't all write a book).

But if we're going to change our mindset long term, if we're going to get this massive societal shift on the road, then I'm afraid it's going to need to be a team effort.

Like I said, we need to open-source this stuff. Between brands and retailers, governments and NGOs, but also on a local level, person-to-person. On social media, at the bus stop, in the changing rooms and in the festival loo queues, we need to be raving about our secondhand finds, applauding the outfit-repeaters, offering to mend each other's buttons. It feels like the best way to keep fashion as an expression of culture and creativity, not a contract we're bound into against our will. Sharing is caring, and collaboration is the best chance we have of taking on the shady conglomerates, calling out the exploiters, championing the little guys, borrowing that killer outfit, locating that magical charity shop, getting our skirt hemmed, discovering an ocean-friendly fabric, helping that lovely social enterprise get off the ground and finding out how to get the gravy stain out of our (massive societal) shift dress. No one person can do it all perfectly, but between us all, we could have this covered.

I hope you'll use this book as a springboard for your own imperfect journey. Like that friend, the one who yelled 'DUMP THEM' while pouring tequila into your coffee mug, I can't promise I know exactly what will happen next – but I am entirely convinced you deserve better than the toxic relationship you're in right now. We all do. The planet does.

And there are still going to be plenty of great outfits in your future, trust me. There are great outfits already in your wardrobe.

So, to summarise: start your shopping ban, Anne. Give mending a go, Jo. Unsubscribe your email, Gail. Just listen to me.

Learn to upcycle, Michael. Count thirty wears, Claire. Ask who made your clothes, Rose. Just get yourself free.

THE WHAT NEXT?
DIRECTORY

Read

Lucy Siegle, *To Die For: Is Fashion Wearing Out the World?*, 2011

Elizabeth L. Cline, *Overdressed: The Shockingly High Cost of Cheap Fashion*, 2012

Tansy E. Hoskins, *Stitched Up: The Anti-Capitalist Book of Fashion*, 2014

Tamsin Blanchard, *Green is the New Black: How to Save the World in Style*, 2007

Vicky Silverthorn, *Start with Your Sock Drawer: The Simple Guide to Living a Less Cluttered Life*, 2016

Barry Schwartz, *The Paradox of Choice: Why More Is Less*, 2005

Click

Fashion Revolution
fashionrevolution.org

Good On You
goodonyou.eco

Labour Behind the Label
labourbehindthelabel.org

Clean Clothes Campaign
cleanclothes.org

Love Your Clothes
loveyourclothes.org.uk

Eco Age
eco-age.com

Stories Behind Things
storiesbehindthings.com

Global Organic Textile Standard
global-standard.org

WRAP
wrap.org.uk

Love Not Landfill
lovenotlandfill.org

Watch

The True Cost, 2015 (Netflix)

Alex James: Slowing Down Fast Fashion, 2016 (Amazon Prime)

Closing the Loop, 2018 (Amazon Prime)

Listen

Clothes & The Rest

Conscious Chatter
Wardrobe Crisis
The Drop

Shop

Mamoq
mamoq.com

Know The Origin
knowtheorigin.com

Gather & See
gatherandsee.com

The Keep
thekeepboutique.com

Lowie
ilovelowie.com

Rêve En Vert
reve-en-vert.com

Thrift+
thrift.plus

Oxfam
oxfam.org.uk/shop

ASOS Marketplace
marketplace.asos.com

Sell

Depop
depop.com

Vestiaire Collective
vestiairecollective.com

HEWI London
hardlyeverwornit.com

Vinted
vinted.co.uk

Facebook Marketplace
facebook.com/marketplace

Rent

HURR Collective
hurrcollective.com

Onloan
onloan.co

My Wardrobe HQ
mywardrobehq.com

Girl Meets Dress
girlmeetsdress.com

ByRotation
byrotation.com

Nuw
thenuwardrobe.com

Repair

Clothes Doctor
clothes-doctor.com

The Restory
the-restory.com

Donate

TRAID
traid.org.uk

Love Not Landfill
lovenotlandfill.org

Thrift+
thrift.plus

ReGAIN
regain-app.com

THANKS A MILLION

Writing this book was a lesson (another one) in the power of the right ensemble. Thank you to the many, many people who have mucked in to help me and educate me over the past year, whether it was their job to or not.

Huge thanks to my editor, Anna, for trusting me with this project, Marie Kondo-ing it beautifully and not letting your memories of my wardrobe circa 2007 put you off. Thank you to Sophie for your clever, thoughtful edits and for catching every place my words were tucked into my metaphorical knickers. Thanks to Jessica, Ellie and the rest of the team at Headline for all your enthusiasm, hard work and brilliant ideas. And thanks as ever to Jemima, for cheering me on and inspiring me to stop hemming things with superglue.

I'm so grateful to all the activists, academics, entrepreneurs and advocates who generously shared their thoughts and expertise with me, and never once made me feel like a terrible person. In no particular order: Sophie Slater, Bronwyn Seier, Dr Dion Terrelonge, Maria Chenoweth, Alex Stedman, Dr Mark Sumner, Laura Von Behr, Charlotte Newland, Emma

Slade Edmonson, Jade Doherty, Victoria Prew, Natalie Hasseck, Holly Bullock, Vicky Silverthorn, Grace Victory, Lauren Cowdery, Jazmin Lee, Neliana Fuenmayor, Mark Chapman, Ellen Robinson, Mandie Voukanari, Bethany Rutter, Siobhan Wilson, Hannah Elliman, Sophie Benson, Rachel Clowes, Tania Arrayales and Tolmeia Gregory. Thanks especially to Aja Barber, for your generous help and insight, and to my Princess Layer, Caroline Jones, for spilling your secrets and reminding me to take things s l o w.

It's only right to say thank you to all the incredible organisations and campaigners across the world who are working so hard right now to turn the juggernaut around. Special thanks to Mary Creagh MP and the Environmental Audit Committee, for all your hard work putting fashion and sustainability on the national agenda, and for creating a definitive report that made my research for this book a *much* less overwhelming task.

Thanks to all the great editors who have kindly commissioned me – in many ways, a stubbornly unfashionable writer – to write about fashion. Particular thanks to all at The Pool (RIP) for my Wardrobe Stories column, a little of which I have lovingly upcycled into this book.

Thank you to everyone at Shop from Crisis Finsbury Park, for all your amazing work and for letting me sing behind the counter.

To Daisy, my #notnewyear compadre – thank you for everything, and not least for the perfect hashtag. Yours is my favourite roast chicken.

Thank you to Sarah, Lizzie, Hannah, Rose and Jo, my Ace Gang, for all your love and support and for not mocking my vintage stylings the first time round.

Thanks to Amy and Ashley, for always having the answers I need to hear and the infant cuddles to go with them.

To my lovely parents, charity shoppers extraordinaire, for showing me the joy of old things (I don't mean you). Thanks to Tom and Dan, who can work a vintage shirt better than anyone, and to my fabulous Granny, for the jumper, the coat, and the tireless PR campaign among the care home staff of Worthing.

To Matt, who is a model of sustainable consumption without even trying. Thank you for the love, always, and for proving it's possible to lead a rich life with only one pair of jeans.

To all of my friends, my family and anyone who has showed an interest in this project – thank you, and I'm sorry if I've ruined shopping for you for ever.

But here's hoping I've made it slightly better.

REFERENCES

1   *Oxford English Dictionary*

2   *Euromonitor International Apparel & Footwear 2016 Edition (volume sales trends 2005–2015)*, 2016

3   Dave Jamieson, Emran Hossain and Kim Bhasin, 'How Bangladesh Garment Industry Traded Workplace Safety For Jobs', *Huffington Post*, 2013

4   WRAP, *Valuing Our Clothes: the cost of UK fashion*, 2017

5   #MyBarnardosDonation campaign, Barnardo's, 2015

6   https://www.barnardos.org.uk/news/barnardos-calls-people-think-pre-loved-buying-new-clothes

7   Waitrose & Partners, *The Waitrose & Partners Food & Drink Report 2018—19: The era of the mindful consumer*, 2019

8   GlobalWebIndex, *Sustainable Packaging Unwrapped*, 2019, https://www.globalwebindex.com/hubfs/Downloads/Sustainable-Packaging-Unwrapped.pdf

9   Mary Quant, *Quant by Quant*, V&A Publishing; Reprint edition, 2012

10 vam.ac.uk/articles/biba

11 Ibid.

12 Barbara Hulanicki interviewed by Lizzie Crocker, 'Barbara Hulanicki, Queen of Fast Fashion', *The Daily Beast*, 2014

13 Environmental Audit Committee, *Fixing fashion: clothing*

consumption and sustainability, Sixteenth Report of Session 2017–19, 2019

14 https://www.forbes.com/sites/gregpetro/2012/10/25/the-future-of-fashion-retailing-the-zara-approach-part-2-of-3/#79271b8f7aa4

15 Andrew Morgan, *The True Cost*, 2015

16 Richard Attenborough, *Gandhi*, 1982

17 https://www.devex.com/news/what-will-move-the-needle-for-worker-well-being-in-the-fashion-industry-88700

18 https://www.theguardian.com/world/2015/mar/12/marks-and-spencer-gap-h-and-m-adidas-cambodian-factories-workers-rights

19 theguardian.com/business/2017/jun/25/female-cambodian-garment-workers-mass-fainting

20 Jenny Holdcroft, IndustriALL, *SPECIAL REPORT: Industry bargaining is an essential tool in the fight for living wages*, 2015

21 Walk Free Foundation, *The Global Slavery Index*, 2018

22 Morgan, *The True Cost*

23 labourbehindthelabel.org/campaigns/living-wage/

24 National Crime Records Bureau Ministry of Home Affairs, 'Accidental Deaths & Suicides in India', 2015

25 China Labor Watch, *The Long March: Survey and Case Studies of Work Injuries in the Pearl River Delta Region*, 2007

26 Fashion Revolution, *The 2 Euro T-Shirt - A Social Experiment*, 2015

27 McKinsey & Company, *The State of Fashion 2019: A year of awakening*, 2018

28 labourbehindthelabel.org

29 Ibid.

30 CARE International, *'I know I cannot quit.': The Prevalence and Productivity Cost of Sexual Harassment to the Cambodian Garment Industry*, March 2017

31 *The Fashion Spot,* 'Fall 2019 Runway Diversity Report: Racial and Age Diversity Step Forward, Size and Gender Inclusivity Step Back', 2019

32 Vandana Shiva, *Earth Democracy: Justice, Sustainability and Peace,* 2005, Zed Books

33 Intergovernmental Panel on Climate Change, Global Warming of 1.5°C, 2019

34 Intergovernmental Panel on Climate Change, Global Warming of 1.5°C, 2019

35 Ellen MacArthur Foundation, *A New Textiles Economy: Redesigning Fashion's Future,* 2017

36 World Wildlife Fund, 'Handle with Care: Understanding the hidden environmental costs of cotton', 2014

37 worldwildlife.org/threats/water-scarcity

38 *Stacey Dooley Investigates: Fashion's Dirty Secrets*, BBC, 2018

39 World Health Organization, *Preventing disease through healthy environments: a global assessment of the burden of disease from environmental risks,* 2016

40 Changing Markets, *Dirty Fashion: How pollution in the global textiles supply chain is making viscose toxic,* 2017

41 https://www.theguardian.com/commentisfree/2016/apr/03/rana-plaza-campaign-handm-recycling

42 wrap.org.uk/content/clothing-waste-prevention

43 #MyBarnardosDonation campaign, Barnardo's, 2015

44 traid.org.uk/23percent

45 Ibid.

46 James Gustave Speth, 'Towards a New Economy and a New Politics', *Solutions,* vol.1, issue 5, 2010, cited in Tansy Hoskins, *Stitched Up: the Anti-Capitalist Book of Fashion,* 2014, Pluto Press

47 Ellen MacArthur Foundation, *A New Textiles Economy: Redesigning Fashion's Future,* 2017

48 McKinsey & Company, *Style that's sustainable: A new fast-fashion formula*, 2016

49 Global Fashion Agenda and The Boston Consulting Group, *Pulse of the Fashion Industry 2017*, 2017

50 United Nations, *Sustainable Development Goals*, 'Goal 12: Ensure sustainable consumption and production patterns', 2015

51 Kirchain, R., Olivetti, E., Reed Miller, T. & Greene, S., Materials Systems Laboratory, Massachusetts Institute of Technology, 'Sustainable Apparel Materials', 2015

52 World Wildlife Fund, 'Handle with Care: Understanding the hidden environmental costs of cotton', 2014

53 Global Fashion Agenda and The Boston Consulting Group, *Pulse of the Fashion Industry 2017*, 2017

54 labourbehindthelabel.org

55 fashionunited.uk

56 Hult Research and Ethical Trading Initiative, *Corporate Leadership on Modern Slavery*, 2016

57 Jenny Holdcroft, IndustriALL, *SPECIAL REPORT: Industry bargaining is an essential tool in the fight for living wages*, 2015

58 Deloitte Access Economics for Oxfam Australia, *A Living Wage in Australia's Clothing Supply Chain: Estimating factory wages as a share of Australia's retail price*, 2017

59 *The Guilty Feminist*, episode 30, 'Ethical Clothing with Aisling Bea', 2017

60 http://labourbehindthelabel.org/campaigns/living-wage/

61 Feargal McGuinness, 'Poverty in the UK: statistics', House of Commons Library, 2018

62 Fashion Revolution, *Fashion Transparency Index 2019; Fashion Transparency Index 2018; Fashion Transparency Index 2017*, 2019, 2018 and 2017

63 https://directory.goodonyou.eco/brand/whistles

64 Environmental Audit Committee, *Fixing fashion: clothing consumption and sustainability* Sixteenth Report of Session 2017–19, 'Appendix: Research by Dr Mark Sumner, School of Design, University of Leeds', 2019

65 Fashion Revolution, *Fashion Transparency Index 2019*, 2019

66 Burberry PLC, *Annual Report 2017/18,* https://www.burberryplc.com/content/dam/burberry/corporate/Investors/Results_Reports/2018/Burberry_AnnualReporT_FY17-18.pdf

67 Dr Nik Hammer, The University of Leicester and the Ethical Trading Initiative, *A New Industry on a Skewed Playing Field: Supply Chain Relations and Working Conditions in UK Garment Manufacturing*, 2015

68 Sarah O'Connor, 'Dark factories: labour exploitation in Britain's garment industry', *Financial Times*, 2018

69 Oxfam, *Reward Work, Not Wealth*, 2018

70 Caitlin Moran, *How To Be a Woman*, 2012, Ebury

71 Barry Schwartz, *The Paradox of Choice: Why More Is Less: Revised Edition*, 2005, Harper Perennial

72 Peter Schofield, Agata Maccarrone-Eaglen, Sheffield Hallam University, 'A cross-cultural and cross-gender analysis of compulsive buying behaviour's core dimensions', *International Journal of Consumer Studies*, volume 42, issue 1

73 Peter Schofield, 'Compulsive shopping is a serious addiction and it's on the rise, study says', *iNews*, 2018

74 William Morris, 'The Beauty of Life', *Hopes and Fears for Art: Five Lectures Delivered in Birmingham, London, and Nottingham, 1878—1881*, 1882, Ellis & White

75 Barry Schwartz, *The Paradox of Choice: Why More Is Less: Revised Edition*, 2005, Harper Perennial

76 Richard Hyman, as quoted in 'Retailers "left behind" as consumers change habits', *BBC News*, 2017

77 Werner Sombart, 'Wirtschaft und Mode', 1902, cited in Tansy

Hoskins, *Stitched Up: the Anti-Capitalist Book of Fashion*, 2014, Pluto Press

78 Episerver, *Reimagining Commerce: Principles of Standout Digital Shopping Experiences*, 2019

79 Personal interview, April 2019

80 'I want to tilt the lens' – Sinéad Burke's fight to make fashion more diverse', *The Guardian*, 2019

81 Luz Claudio, 'Waste Couture: Environmental Impact of the Clothing Industry', *Environmental Health Perspective*, 2007

82 Caitlin Moran, *How To Be a Woman*, Ebury, 2012

83 Ethical Consumer, *Ethical Consumer Markets Report 2018*, 2018

84 Andrew Morgan, *The True Cost*, 2015

85 Personal interview, April 2019

86 Orsola de Castro, via instagram.com/fash_rev https://www.instagram.com/p/Bwlqq0_h7kD/

87 Frida Kahlo and Carlos Fuentes, The Diary of Frida Kahlo: An Intimate Self-Portrait, 1995, Bloomsbury Publishing PLC

88 Princeton University Neuroscience Institute, 'Interactions of top-down and bottom-up mechanisms in human visual cortex', *The Journal of Neuroscience*, 2011

89 Catherine A. Roster, Joseph R. Ferrari, Martin Peter Jurkat, 'The dark side of home: Assessing possession "clutter" on subjective well-being', *Journal of Environmental Psychology*, 2016

90 Mark Twain, *The Jumping Frog: And 18 Other Stories*, 2000, Book Tree

91 Joan Crawford, *My Way of Life*, Simon & Schuster, 1971

92 AEG, *Care Label Project*, 2017

93 Chris Tyree and Dan Morrison, Orb Media, *INVISIBLES: The plastic inside us*, 2017

94 Mike Berners-Lee and Duncan Clark, 'What's the carbon footprint of . . . a load of laundry?', *The Guardian*, 2010

95 thereformation.com/pages/wash-smart

96 WRAP, *Valuing Our Clothes: the cost of UK fashion*, 2017

97 *Friends*, 'The One With The Flashback', 1996, Warner Bros.

98 Jane Milburn, *Slow Clothing: Finding Meaning in What We Wear*, 2017, Textile Beat

99 As quoted by Zoe Wood, 'A stitch in time – new era for home sewing', *The Guardian*, 2017

100 Ibid.

101 Quoted from Sofie Hagen's *Made of Human* podcast, 'Episode 136. Bethany Rutter #2 - Thorny Difficultness of Being Fat', 2019

102 Fashion Revolution, Fanzine #004 *Fashion Craft Revolution*, 2019

103 Gilda Radner, *It's Always Something*, Simon & Schuster, 20th Anniversary, Revised edition, 2009

104 Pina Bausch, quoted in Kisselgoff, A., 'Pina Bausch Dance: Key Is Emotion', *The New York Times*, 1985

105 Elizabeth L. Cline, *Overdressed: The Shockingly High Cost of Cheap Fashion*, 2012, Penguin

106 Mignon McLaughlin, *Aperçus: The Aphorisms of Mignon McLaughlin*, 2014, The Brabant Press

107 Ariel, *The Great British Wardrobe Report*, 2017

108 Iris Apfel, *Iris*, Albert Maysles, 2014

109 Amy Heckerling, *Clueless*, 1995

110 John Berger, *Ways of Seeing*, 1972, Penguin

111 https://www.forbes.com/sites/gregpetro/2012/10/25/the-future-of-fashion-retailing-the-zara-approach-part-2-of-3/#7f55204f7aa4

112 *Absolutely Fabulous*, season three, episode four, 'Jealous', BBC, 1992

113 Alice Wilby, quoted in Fashion Revolution Fanzine issue 2, *Loved Clothes Last*, 2017

114 Fashion Revolution, *Fashion Transparency Index 2019*, 2019

115 Ibid., 2019, 2018 and 2017

116 Ibid., 2019

117 Ibid.

118 about.hm.com/en/sustainability/sustainable-fashion/materials/cotton.html

119 Dr Bettina Musiolek, *Clean Clothes Campaign, H&M: fair living wages were promised, poverty wages are the reality*, 2018

120 Ibid.

121 https://www.fashionrevolution.org/2018-impact/

122 Ibid.

123 fashionrevolution.org/about/get-involved

124 Safia Minney, ''Fair trade is a slow process', *The Guardian*, 2008

125 goodonyou.eco/how-ethical-is-marks-spencer

126 Summer Rayne Oakes, *Style, Naturally,* 2008, Chronicle Books

127 Lyst, *Year in Fashion 2018*, 2018

128 As quoted by Zoe Wood in 'Boohoo sales soar after taking "fashion for all" approach', *The Guardian*, 2019

129 The phenomenon named for the 2016 viral tweet by Australian cartoonist Ben Ward: 'The whole internet loves Milkshake Duck, a lovely duck that drinks milkshakes! *5 seconds later* We regret to inform you the duck is racist.'

130 As quoted in 'The Future of Fashion is Sustainable', *Thailand Tatler*, 2018

131 Nielsen, *Nielsen Global Corporate Sustainability Report*, 2015

132 https://www.nimblefins.co.uk/average-cost-school-uniform

133 https://wwd.com/business-news/business-features/zaras-green-agenda-zero-waste-100-sustainable-fabrics-1203220857/

134 As quoted in Elizabeth Gaskell, *The Life of Charlotte Brontë*, 1998, Penguin Classics; new edition

135 https://techcrunch.com/2019/03/21/rent-the-runway-hits-a-1-billion-valuation/

136 The Carbon Trust, *International Carbon Flows*, 2011, https://www.carbontrust.com/resources/reports/advice/international-carbon-flows/

137 ThredUp, ThredUp 2019 Resale Report, 2019

138 Figures direct from Depop, May 2019

139 Sarah Butler, "Everyone I know buys vintage": the Depop sellers shaking up fashion', *The Guardian*, 2018

140 Henry David Thoreau, *Walden*, 1854, Ticknor and Fields

141 ThredUp, *ThredUp 2019 Resale Report, 2019*

142 Homer, *The Odyssey*, 1983, Outlet

143 Charity Retail Association, *Charity Retail Association 2018 Research Programme*, 2018

144 Richard Blackburn, *Sustainable Textiles: Life Cycle and Environmental Impact*, Woodhead Publishing, 2009

145 Sophie Benson, 'Where Do Your Charity Shop Donations Really Go?', *Grazia Daily*, 2019

146 Fashion Revolution, 'Manifesto for a Fashion Revolution', point no.10

147 Global Fashion Agenda, Boston Consulting Group and Sustainable Apparel Coalition, *Pulse of the Fashion Industry 2019 Update*, 2019

148 *Work Like a Woman by Mary Portas*, episode two: 'Embracing Failure with Elizabeth Day', 2019

149 https://about.hm.com/en/media/news/financial-reports/2019/4/3275581.html

INDEX